Tramping in
New Zealand

Margo Falls

Tramping in New Zealand

Published by
    Lonely Planet Publications
    PO Box 88, South Yarra
    Victoria 3141, Australia

Printed by
    Colorcraft
    Hong Kong

Photographs by
    NZ Government Tourist Board (cover)
    Jim DuFresne (all others)

First published
    November 1982

Jim DuFresne is a freelance writer, specialising in outdoor and travel writing. For much of the year he lives in Juneau, Alaska, and has hiked extensively throughout Alaska and the Canadian and American Rockies. Before writing this book, Jim spent several months in New Zealand and completed many of the country's major tracks.

National Library of Australia
    Cataloguing-in-Publication Data

DuFresne, Jim.
    Tramping in New Zealand.

    ISBN 0 908086 33 4.

    1. New Zealand — Description and travel — 1951 —
    Guide-books. I. Title.

919.31'0437

© Jim DuFresne, 1982

All rights reserved. No part of this publication may be reproduced, stored in a retrieval system or transmitted in any form by any means, electronic, mechanical, photocopying, recording or otherwise, except brief extracts for the purpose of review, without the written permission of the publisher and copyright owner.

Acknowledgments

A book, any book, is written by one but made possible by many. Mine is no less. The number of people who had an idea, a say or a helping hand in putting this book together would fill the telephone directory of Halfmoon Bay, Stewart Island.

Warm affection goes to my travelling and tramping partners Richard Greybill and Mike 'Am I Supposed to Be Here' Cowan who endured many rugged treks and misconnections with me. Especially Cowan who demonstrated that, yes, you can take a trip at the last minute without any previous arrangements.

New Zealanders were warm-hearted and extremely hospitable during my long stay. Keith Wilson, Ruth Kiddie and A Fish of the New Zealand Alpine Club gave me their time and years of experience while the rangers and employees of the Lands and Survey map room and the NZ Forest Service Office in Auckland went out of their way to supply me with the most current information. Mrs Halls, whose fine bed and breakfast I stayed at in Auckland, inspired me daily with Shakespeare recitations during early morning tea.

In the United States I was grateful for editorial assistance from many people, especially Patty Ginsburg, Jeff Sloss and Lori Evans. Many borrowed typewriters were used to pound out the first draft and I will be forever indebted to Ken Leghorn, Bonnie Kaden and the rest of the *Alaska Discovery* gang, and to Joel Bennet, for the use of offices and typewriters.

I must give thanks to Todd Hardesty for his late night rejuvenation, John Manly for his artistic touch and my folks for enduring a son who travels extensively, writes much but makes little. And to Sue Christian and Jeff Sloss who tipped me off to the fine tramping in New Zealand and encouraged me to go. But most of all to Peggy — my harshest critic, my toughest editor, my most loyal supporter, my wife.

Jim DuFresne

Publisher's Acknowledgement — and a request
Jim DuFresne wrote this book in Juneau, Alaska immediately after his tour of New Zealand and his exploration of its tramping tracks. His manuscript was edited by David Sidwell of Auckland, a former National Park ranger, following a check of every section of senior rangers in national parks and state forests. Particular thanks are due to T Cookson (Thames), G A Mitchell (Murupara), J C Clay (New Plymouth), R Goldring (Turangi), M C Reedy, B E Jefferies (Mt Ruapehu), G J A Grieg (Masterton), G Rennison (Takaka), M Clarbrough (St Arnaud), NZ Forest Service (Hanmer Springs), C J

Stewart (Mt Cook), W F Hislop (Wanaka), P M Green (Invercargill) and R Tindal (Stewart Island).

These officers checked the text and provided supplementary information. While responsibility for the content of the book rests with the author and publisher, trampers and travellers are advised that their safety in the forests and mountains requires consultation with the regional officers for current maps and route conditions, and caution in planning each journey.

All Lonely Planet travel guides are updated regularly. To do this we need up-to-date information, so if you find something that would improve future editions of this book, write and tell us. Good letters are rewarded with a free copy of the next edition, or another Lonely Planet guide if you prefer.

LONELY PLANET NEWSLETTER

We collect an enormous amount of information here at Lonely Planet. Apart from our research we also get a steady stream of letters from people out on the road — some of them are just one line on a postcard, others go on for pages. Plus we always have an ear to the ground for the latest on cheap airfares, new visa regulations, borders opening and closing. A lot of this information goes into our new editions or 'update supplements' in reprints. But we'd like to make better use of this information so we are now producing a quarterly newsletter packed full of the latest news from out on the road. It appears in February, May, August and November of each year. If you'd like an airmailed copy of the most recent newsletter just send us A$1.50 (A$1 within Australia) or A$5 (A$4 in Australia) for a year's subscription.

Contents

Why New Zealand?

The answer came to me while sitting on the Harris Saddle, high above the bushline on the Routeburn Track. But it was neither from meditation nor did the heavens suddenly open up and send it down. It came from a Kiwi, a veteran New Zealand tramper, who was there when I arrived, gazing out at the endless view of valleys, mountains and lakes before him.

The question that was bothering me: What makes New Zealand such a paradise for trampers and backpackers? His answer: 'It's all here, mate. We have the oceans, the lakes, the hot pools and the cold streams. There are mountain peaks covered by snow, lush rain forests filled with waterfalls an dry deserts with nothing. We have trees by the hectares, glaciers by the dozens, fish by the millions. We have it all except one thing.'

'What's missing?'

'The crowds.'

So true. In the time I spent tramping in this country, rarely were the facilities bulging at the seams with users. Never was my tranquility with nature disturbed by hoards of people rushing through. If there is such a thing as a tramper's paradise, this special land in the South Pacific is the closest place to it.

New Zealand, a country of about 270,000 sq. km from tip to toe, or two-thirds of the size of California, has a population of a little more than three million. California has close to 23 million. The difference during the summer between Yosemite National Park in California and the Nelson Lakes area in the South Island . . . well, there are no similarities. One has trails over-run with hikers and families, campgrounds overfilled with tents and trailers. The other has room to breathe, isolated spots to seek out, or lonely mountain peaks to climb and name. Both have spectacular scenery. But in New Zealand you tramp for two important reasons: to be one in nature by becoming part of it, and to lose sight of man's doings — of cars and buildings and people and pollution — by getting away from it all. As one Kiwi remarked, 'Ten minutes into the bush and you can't hear a thing. You might as well be a 100 miles from civilisation.'

Occasionally a track, especially the famous Milford, will have people on it most of the summer. Some will only have trampers during the holiday season, and many will seem virtually deserted all the time. But none, even the highly regulated Milford, will be overflowing with families and dogs and boy scout troops. Not by Yosemite Park standards. Neither will they have the appearance as if a 50th class reunion was just held, with trash and beer bottles, cut trees and fire pits scattered about.

The lack of crowds is just one reason why New Zealand could rightfully be labelled a tramper's paradise. From the words of the old Kiwi — it's all there. You are able to choose they type of hiking that is most appealing in the type of terrain most inspiring. There are tracks that go through lush green rain forests where in every bend of the trail a waterfall is tumbling down the mountain side. There are tracks that weave along golden beaches, around smoking volcanoes, or over streams that hordes of miners once hunched over with gold pans.

Some tracks are cut, marked, benched, and even have mile signs along them. Some are nothing more than an occasional orange tag or cairn of rocks along a river bed or mountain ridge. And there is everything in between for whatever amount of physical exertion you feel like putting out.

The development of tracks and their facilities are the result of a great interest in tramping by the government and the public. Next to rugby and horse racing (and possibly beer drinking), tramping can be considered one of the country's greatest national pastimes. The Federated Mountain Clubs of New Zealand is an organization of over 50 tramping and mountaineering clubs, whose thousands of members use the fine system of tracks and huts on a constant basis. Undoubtedly thousands more, individuals or families unaffiliated with any particular tramping group, also venture into the back-country for a first-hand look at their country's natural beauty and wonders.

Tracks are plentiful in New Zealand and, just as important, they are easy to get to. If you have a car you can reach most major tracks along reasonably good roads. If you don't, there is a good system of public transportation that will get you there or at least somewhere close to the head of the trail. From there rangers, park wardens or other trampers are usually friendly enough to give you a lift. A little planning is sometimes needed to get back to a vehicle but rarely is there a need to charter expensive airplanes or float planes to the backcountry as in much of Alaska or northern Canada.

Also there is not the distance between good trails as in many large countries. From the end of one track it is never more than an hour or two to the beginning of the next one. For all its variety, New Zealand is an amazingly compact country, which is good for trampers. You spend your time trekking, not riding the public bus.

Backpackers couldn't ask for a better climate. There is still a need to prepare for unpredictable, foul weather, but overall New Zealand's climate is mild without great variations in temperatures or changes in season. In the north you can hike in sunshine or subtropical temperatures, but without the blistering heat of northern Australia. In the south there are fall colours or a layer of snow on an early spring morning, but not the extreme cold of northern United States or Canada. New Zealand's climate seems to be mildly in the middle.

Trampers can choose their type of weather in this amazing country. There is sunshine along the beaches of Abel Tasman National Park, 5½ metres of rain a year in Fiordland, or both rain and sun on the same afternoon on Stewart Island.

New Zealand is a little short on wildlife. Whether this is a blessing to trampers or something dreadfully missing is debatable. But there is no need to worry about snakes, poisonous insects or a grizzly bear charging you in the middle of the track. One species most of the country possesses in great abundance is trout . . . and the clear lakes and streams the grand fish thrives in. This is good for the fisherman and the tramper.

There is an excess of drinking water along most tracks. Very few times will you need to carry water or purify it from a stream. Only on settled land, bog areas or farmland should it be boiled before drinking. Not only is it pure, but cold, clear and sweet to the taste. Surely some of the finest water in the world is flowing off the mountains in New Zealand.

The tracks in most areas are well maintained and marked by workers from the national parks, state forests or private tramping clubs. There is also a vast network of huts that coincide with the vast number of trails. Huts are very handy to the trampers for it means lighter loads to carry — minus tents, foam rubber mats and camping stoves. They are a good place to dry out your boots or warm up in front of an open fireplace at the end of the day.

THIS BOOK

The tramper is in heaven in New Zealand and the purpose of this book is to open the gates for him. It is an aid for the Kiwi who wants to progress from day hikes to week-long tramps; or the overseas visitor with a limited time schedule. This is not a camping or hiking manual. It will not teach you the proper way to walk or how to set up a tent. For that information you should consult *Bushcraft* (edited by R W Burrell for the National Mountain Safety Council of New Zealand), Grant Hunter's *Tramper's Handbook*, or Tony Nolan's *Bush Lore*.

The intention of this book is to describe the wide variety of tracks and different outings possible in the New Zealand backcountry. It describes the tracks, the terrain, the weather, the highlights and the history. It should be used as a guide to where you want to tramp and what to expect.

These 20 tracks in this book have been chosen for a variety of reasons. All are more than just a day hike. All will take you into the country's scenic wilderness not always possible in a single four-hour trek. They range from an easy three-day walk in the Coromandel State Forest to the enduring 10-day adventure from Lake Hauroko to the West Arm of Lake Manapouri in Fiordland National Park.

They stretch from one end of the country to the other and include all 10 national parks, six state forests and most of the interesting geological features of New Zealand. They are known for their historical or scenic beauty and are frequently used during the summer season. You will not be a trail blazer, rather the tracks will be cut, marked in a variety of ways and easy to follow even for those who are undertaking their first extended trek in the wilderness.

All the tracks have a series of huts to provide good shelter and cooking facilities within four to six hours of each other. Most have easy access to public transport, although a few might take a little extra planning to get to the trailhead before or after the trek. There is little doubling back and many are circular so you finish where you began. And except for the Copland Track, none of them need mountaineering equipment or skills. All of them can be done without hiring guides if the party is prepared, in shape, and has the right equipment.

But most of all, they range in difficulty, lengths and landscape, giving you the best possible selection of New Zealand's natural wonders and scenery.

Included below and in later descriptions are ratings of tracks and the amount of time needed to hike from one point to the next. They are only an average and will not exactly match your expectations or speed. What one tramper thinks is a backbreaking hike, the next will judge as a pleasant walk. No two are alike. Some people like to stroll along, taking pictures and rest stops at every bend. Some like to put their head down and push to the next hut. To each his own. But judge for yourself your own endurance level and your own walking speed (the average is four km per hour on easy, level track) then plan your trip and days accordingly. The walking time allows for appropriate rest periods, five minutes every hour, but not a two-hour tea break in a tussock meadow. I found that weather plays the greatest factor in my walking speed. Somehow when it was rainy, cold and windy I always made it to the next hut in near record time. But when the sun was shining, the skies clear and the temperatures pleasantly warm, I might not make it there till almost nightfall.

Tracks in New Zealand can be classified in three categories — walks, tracks, or routes. Walks are well-formed pathways with bridges over streams, split logs over bog areas and bush regularly cut back along the sides. They are gentle enough for families and the most novice tramper to handle. Tracks are trails that have been cut, marked and should be easy to follow, though at times you might be temporarily confused at a stream bed or on a ridge. They can be attemped by people in a reasonable amount of fitness. Routes are lightly-marked trails, usually indicated by only poles, metal tags or rock cairns, and should be attempted by only well-conditioned, well-equipped hikers who have a few backcountry tramps under their belts.

All 20 hikes in this book fall into the category of tracks although some — Milford, Routeburn, Coromandel State Forest — are so heavily used and maintained that they may almost be classified as walks. Others — Kaimanawa State Forest, Harper Pass Track, Copland — are tracks with an occasional route section over a ridge or along a river bed. For our purpose, the 20 tracks will be rated under three headings: mild, for those that are well used and maintained and could be tackled by trampers with just day hike experience; medium, for those that are well marked but trampers should be in shape and well equipped for the outing; strenuous, for those that should not be taken lightly but can be done by a party with an experienced tramper and the right equipment. All members must be prepared for the hike.

THE TRACKS

1 Coromandel Forest Park (Mild) An easy hike in the North Island along the forested ridges of the Coromandel Range and through the Kauaeranga Valley where logging and gold mining relics are of special interest.

2 Lake Waikaremoana Track (Mild to medium) A tramp around almost the entire lake, the largest body of water in the Urewera National Park. Forest, open ridges and beautiful views of the lake highlight this popular walking track.

3 Whakatane & Waikare Rivers Track (Strenuous) A circular trek along two of the major, and most scenic rivers in upper Urewera National Park in the North Island. Heavily forested valleys and ridges make up the terrain along the track which passes through the historical Maori section of Maungapohatu.

4 Mt Egmont Round-the-Mountain Track (Medium) A popular track around the cone of Mt Egmont in Egmont National Park in the North Island. Bush, beech forest and scenic alpine sections make up the variety of terrain on the trek.

5 Tongariro Round-the-Mountain Track (Medium) A trip past the three major volcanoes and thermal area of Tongariro National Park in the North Island. Almost the entire track is above the bushline, crossing many ridges and including spectacular views of the surrounding valleys. Highlight of the track is the hot springs near one hut.

6 Kaimanawa State Forest Park (Strenuous) A tramp in the rugged forest, a long-time favourite of deer hunters, east of Lake Taupo in the North Island. Most of the track is located in beech forest although two days are spent above the bushline along tussock grasslands in the Kaimanawa Range for two days.

7 Tararua State Forest Park (Strenuous) A trek in the rugged mountain range that has become the playground for Wellington trampers in the North Island. The trail includes tussock grasslands as well as thick beech forests in the lowlands and, like Wellington itself, will probably have spells of windy and rainy weather.

8 Abel Tasman Coastal Track (Mild) One of the best coastal tracks in New Zealand, which works its way along the Tasman Bay in Abel Tasman National Park in the South Island. Scenery includes beautiful bays, beaches and interesting tidal flats. The area is known for its particularly fine weather.

9 Heaphy Track (Mild to medium) Almost as well known as the Milford Track, the Heaphy is situated in the North-West Nelson State Forest in the South Island. The popular but long walk runs from hilly beech forest areas to beautiful coastal beaches on the Tasman Sea.

10 Wangapeka Track (Medium to strenuous) Lying in the same state forest as the Heaphy but not nearly as popular, this track to many trampers is the more scenic and more spectacular of the two. A harder trip overall, the Wangapeka winds through beech forest and over many saddles. Like the Heaphy this track needs careful planning to get in and out of it.

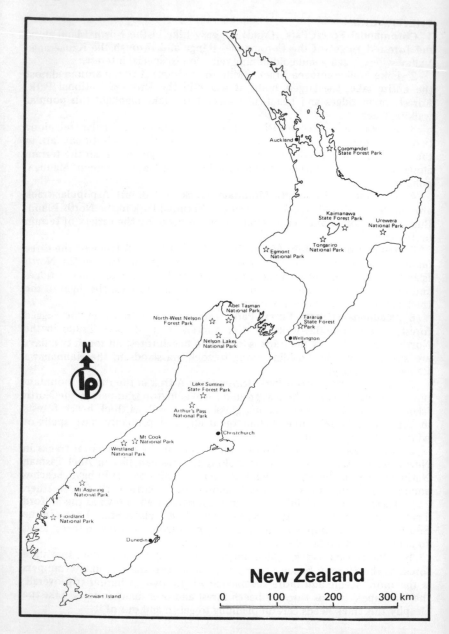

New Zealand

11 Copland Track (Strenuous) A challenging hike from Mt Cook National Park to Westland National Park over the Copland Pass in the Southern Alps. This is the only one where special alpine knowledge and equipment — crampons, ice axe, ropes — are needed. Both equipment and guides can be hired for the trek that includes spectacular alpine scenery, ice fields, beech forests and even hot springs for the weary tramper at one hut.

12 Travers-Sabine Track (Medium to strenuous) Grassy riverbeds, beech forests and an alpine saddle make up the features of this trip in Nelson Lakes National Park in the South Island. The track runs along two major lakes, Rotoiti and Rotoroa, and through the Travers and Sabine Valleys, areas popular with trampers during the summer.

13 Harper Pass Track (Medium to strenuous) A trek which begins in Lake Sumner State Foret and continues over the Harper Pass into Arthur's Pass National Park in the South Island. Historically a passage for Maoris and gold miners, today it is a scenic route for trampers, passing through beech forest and wide river flats.

14 Routeburn Track (Mild) An exceptional variety of sub-alpine scrub and rain forest make this hike in the Mt Aspiring and Fiordland National Parks one of the best in the country. The sheer beauty of the natural surroundings and the well-maintained track mean that many trampers use it throughout the summer.

15 Rees-Dart Track (Medium) A trip along the two great rivers that fall mostly in Mt Aspiring National Park in the South Island. Open grasslands, good views of ranges and possible day hikes to glaciers highlight the tramp.

16 Greenstone-Caples Track (Medium) Although not as scenic or popular as the Routeburn, this walk through the two valleys is less crowded and offers its own beauty in rain forests and groves of thick beech. The Greenstone is also a means to return to Queenstown after the Routeburn.

17 Milford Track (Mild) Undoubtedly the best known and most heavily used track in New Zealand. It runs from the end of Lake Te Anau to the Milford Sound in the Fiordland National Park. It offers a wide variety of rain forest, alpine meadows and spectacular waterfalls. Special arrangements are needed, however, as reservations, launch trips and hut permits must be made in advance during the busy summer.

18 Hollyford Track (Medium to strenuous) A tramp through rain forest, past Lake McKerrow and out to isolated Martins Bay on the west coast. The track lies in the Fiordland National Park and feature superb trout and coastal fishing, good mountain views and interesting seal and penguin colonies.

19 Lake Hauroko—Supper Cove—West Arm (Strenuous) At the other end of the Fiordland National Park is this track which offers the isolation and solitude the Milford cannot. A rugged track but very scenic. Special arrangements have to be made with boat launches as it begins and ends on isolated lake shores.

20 Stewart Island (Strenuous) Off by itself, this island is a tramper's delight with a wide system of tracks that offers impressive scenery of bays and isolated beaches. The mud and bog make it difficult but the track and native birdlife is well worth getting your boots dirty.

These are just brief descriptions of the tracks covered in detail in the following chapters. Many can be done together as some trampers go from the Routeburn directly to the Greenstone or the Hollyford, or complete the Heaphy and head back to Nelson by means of the Wangapeka. In doing so, however, you must be careful of your supplies, the amount you carry and where you can purchase additional food items. Other tracks need not be done in their entirety but rather only sections that time or experience will permit. This is especially true of the Copland. A common trip on this track is to hike up from the west coast to the first two huts and then double back along the same route, eliminating the divide and the need for special equipment and training.

Before embarking on a track, make sure your equipment, time and experience are sufficient for the outing. While on the track, remember the minimum impact code drawn up by the Nature Conversation Council:

— Small tramping parties are best.
— Plan your outing to minimize rubbish.
— Pack out what you carry in when no facility is provided for disposal.
— Keep to the tracks where they exist.
— Keep campsite construction to a minimum.
— Avoid camping near huts or tracks.
— Do not wash yourself or dishes in the streams with soap.
— Burn or bury all toilet wastes.
— Avoid fires by using portable stoves.
— Conserve all wood when using fires.
— Take special care to protect all native wildlife and flora.

Facts for Trampers

All tracks in New Zealand are controlled by one of three organizations — a national park board, the New Zealand Forest Service, or the Walkway Commission — or owned by private individuals.

There are 10 national parks in New Zealand, three in the North Island and seven in the South Island, administered by the Lands and Survey Department. The Department is responsible for the preservation of each area and controls its use for recreation activities such as tramping, hunting, fishing and skiing. Each park publishes a handbook containing information on history, wildlife, flora, geology, huts and tracks. Maps and other data sheets are published according to need. These publications can be obtained at the park headquarters, usually located in the closest town or village to the main access (check Appendix C for addresses). Before embarking on a track in a national park a quick stop at the headquarters will often reward you with additional information about the track, the latest weather forecast, or any unusual situations that might appear during your trip. On some of the more popular tracks in national parks there are wardens stationed at certain huts to collect fees, maintain trails and perform other duties. They may also be a good source of information about the track, although one should be careful with the information for many have been on the route only as far as their hut.

The national parks and their headquarters are:

North Island:
- Egmont (headquarters at Dawson Falls on Mt Egmont)
- Tongariro (Whakapapa Village on Mt Ruapehu)
- Urewera (Aniwaniwa on Lake Waikaremoana).

South Island:
- Abel Tasman (Totaranui at the west end of the park)
- Nelson Lakes (St Arnaud)
- Westland (Fox)
- Arthur's Pass (Arthur's Pass village)
- Mount Cook (next to the Hermitage Hotel)
- Mt Aspiring (Wanaka)
- Fiordland (Te Anau) — the largest national park.

The New Zealand Forest Service (NZFS) has control over four million hectares of land and eighteen major state forest park but administers them with a different philosophy from that of national park boards. While the boards work to preserve 'an area in its natural state', the NZFS follows the 'multiple-use concept' in its administration of the state forests. In the national parks, everything is secondary to preservation, tramping included. Many state forest parks have no outstanding natural features and are the site of working areas for timber production or other uses.

Still, there is tramping in all of them and some of the country's best-known tracks, including Heaphy and Wangapeka, are located in state forest parks. There are eight regional offices for the NZFS (check Appendix C for addresses) with the largest in downtown Auckland in the Hobson Towers on Federal St. The information centre on the seventh floor has almost every handout the NZFS has ever published. Most are free and have good information about tramping, but you may have to get past the office girl to a ranger in the back before obtaining them. There is also a little-known map room on the fifth floor, where they sell a few state forest maps and keep all of them on file, even some like Kaimanawa State Forest which is out of print at the time of writing.

The New Zealand Walkways Commission was established in 1975 in an effort to form a network of inter-connecting walking tracks which will ultimately provide a continuous path from Cape Reinga at the north end to Bluff in the south. In the beginning its main emphasis has been to provide access for short family outings into the countryside from major urban areas. The 21 walks that were originally set up are mostly day hikes in areas of historical or cultural interest to New Zealanders. For general information on any of the walkways, contact The Secretary, New Zealand Walkway Commission, c/o Department of Lands and Survey, Head Office, Private Bag, Wellington.

To travel through private land on which a track spills over, it is a good practice to obtain permission before undertaking the trip, though at times it might be difficult to locate the owner. On many of the heavily-used tracks, however, the effort is unnecessary as trampers are expected and welcomed.

The department that oversees everyone in New Zealand is Lands and Survey, which has extensive operations in administering 12 million of land or — almost half of New Zealand. One function of the department most important to trampers is the publication of maps, both topographical and recreational. Its largest offices are in Auckland (in the State Insurance Building) and in Wellington (in the Charles Ferguson Building, up the street from the Beehive). There are also good offices in the North Island at Hamilton, Gisborne, Napier, Rotorua, New Plymouth and Whangarei, and in the South Island at Blenheim, Christchurch, Dunedin, Hokitika, Invercargill and Nelson. Maps can also be obtained in stationery shops or outdoor stores but these tend to have only a select few.

The department publishes its topographical maps in three scales: 1:63,360 (one inch to one mile), 1:250,000 and 1:500,000. The less area a map covers, or the smaller the scale, the more detail. Trampers generally use 1:63,360 as it shows tracks, bridges, swamps, ridges or other points of interest. Sometimes, however, the best bet are the recreational maps. Although their scale is generally larger, most of them give track descriptions, hut sizes, interesting side trips and other useful information in the back side. These are the maps that are placed in most huts of the national parks.

HUTS

Like the land you will walk on, the huts you will sleep in are built and controlled by three different groups. The national parks boards build the ones on their tracks, the NZFS the ones on theirs, and tramping clubs seem to have some on both.

Tramping clubs were actually the first to begin building huts on the tracks when they began erecting shelters for their members in the 1920s and '30s. At that time most of the clubs had to leave them open to obtain permission to build on crown land. After the war, the clubs resumed building huts along with several of the national parks which were trying to encourage more public use of the land.

In the 1960s, the NZFS followed suit by erecting huts to promote state forests to the public and increase their recreational use. Some say this was a direct result of a growing rivalry between the NZFS and the national parks. The difference between the two is that the NZFS huts tend to be newer, larger, in better condition, and free to the trampers. National park huts are, of course, older, worn down a little more but still perfectly adequate. At these huts there is usually a warden or an honesty box to collect fees. Fees can be anywhere from 50 cents a night to $3 for the more popular ones.

Most huts have foam rubber mats, cooking facilities which consist of either an open fireplace, wood stove or gas burners, clothes line for drying, tables, benches and a friendly look to them after a long day on the track. They are placed four to five hours apart on the tracks and have a two-night limit when they are full during the holidays. Although it is a good practice to obtain permission to use club huts, shelters in the backcountry are usually left unlocked in case of emergency.

It is a good idea to check with authorities about the conditions of huts before embarking on a track. Huts near the end or the beginning of a track, or which have easy access by a road can be crowded at times and occasionally in very poor shape. Most of the times, however, when bunks become filled, husbands and wives and brothers and sisters double up, or late arrivals make sleeping space on tables and floors. It is especially important to check out the condition of huts above the bushline as many do not have firewood during the busy holiday season or anytime at all, in which case it will pay off to carry a small camp stove and fuel.

There is an honesty box in many huts for donations and an honesty system in all to help keep them clean. This means sweeping the floor, emptying the ashes from stoves or fireplaces, replacing split wood and packing out your cans and garbage. After a tiring five-hour hike, the last thing you want to come to is a dirty hut with no split firewood.

Camping on many of the tracks, especially the popular ones in national parks, is prohibited. On certain trails, such as the Milford and Routeburn, the wardens are very strict about this and for good reason. With perhaps 7000 trampers on the track every year, strict hut usage is the only way to prevent old campsites and smoking fire pits appearing on every inch of the route. Most of the tracks in the state forest allow camping and a tent is often a good item to carry during the holidays.

On many tracks, especially those in the South Island, the huts serve another important purpose for trampers — a safe and dry shelter to wait out a day of bad weather. New Zealand weather in the backcountry is famous for being unstable, unpredictable and uncompromising when you are on a limited time schedule. It is best to work in a free day in all trips for the chance you might be caught in a spell of rain, wind, or even snow.

WEATHER

The usual pattern of weather in New Zealand is one of high pressure fronts travelling west to east, followed by low pressure systems. The high pressure systems give you the beautiful fair weather while the low pressure systems (also called troughs or depressions) bring the rain and cold temperatures. An early warning sign for the bad weather is an increase in wind and the appearance of high cloud sheets known as 'hog's back' on the lee side of the mountains. These clouds are a good indication that strong winds and high humidity are on their way. As the trough closes in, clouds will thicken and rain may develop. If the low pressure system has a depression centre, winds up to gale force or greater may develop, bringing with them heavy rain, snow or even blizzards. It is important to realize that snowfalls and blizzards can occur in the mountains at any time of the year and not just during the winter when the skiers are praying for snow.

Once the low pressure system moves away, the wind will change directions, often quite suddenly, with westerlies changing to southerlies or northerlies to westerlies. Eventually another high pressure system will move in and fine weather will return.

All mountain chains in New Zealand run in a line from north or northeast to south or south-west, acting as a natural barrier to the normal direction of air flow. Thus the air is forced to rise over the ranges, creating more bad weather and stronger winds on the mountains than anywhere else. Alpine hikers usually get more foul weather than those who are tramping in valleys or lowlands. It is not uncommon to have bad weather in the lowlands of the windward or western side of the ranges, fine weather on the lee side and miserable conditions on both sides of the ridges in the middle. It's the price you pay for all those spectacular views from alpine tramping.

In case of bad weather, it is best to wait it out in the comfort and safety of a hut. But if you do have to hike out, be especially cautious of rapidly rising rivers. Rain or snow in the mountains will cause streams and rivers to flood extremely quickly, especially in the spring when the rain is falling on soft snowfields. If the river is too high or moving too fast, then search for a wire crossing or swing bridge in the area or wait for the level to drop.

The New Zealand Meteorological Service gives general forecasts, covering the entire country, at regular intervals on national radio programmes, while local stations broadcast forecasts for the surrounding area. On some stations special mountain forecasts are broadcast on Fridays for trampers, hunters, climbers and skiers. You can obtain these mountain reports for any area by contacting the nearest meteorological office. There are forecast offices at the Auckland, Wellington, Ohakea and Christchurch airports where the predictions are prepared. There are also briefing offices at the Kaitaia, Whenuapai, Rotorua, Gisborne, New Plymouth, Paraparaumu, Nelson, Wigram (Christchurch), Dunedin and Invercargill airports, and at Waiouru and Kaikoura. They can give you information about any region's upcoming weather. A good handout worth reading is 'Weather Wisdom In New Zealand Mountains' published by the Mountain Safety Council as a guide for trampers and climbers. It's free and can be picked up at most national park headquarters.

WHEN TO GO

Most national parks and state forests experience their largest influx of trampers during the Christmas school holidays, from mid-December to the end of January. This is when Kiwis have extended vacation time and the weather in most aress is at its best. Most tracks, including the twenty in this book, can be undertaken any time from early December through March with the expectation of a few nice days and reasonably mild temperatures. Some tracks in the North Island and a few in the north-west section of the South Island can be tackled in April or November. The months of June, July and August are for winter hiking where special skills and equipment are needed to combat cold temperatures, snow and strong winds. March and November can also be especially chilly and wet months for the tracks in the Fiordland area or Stewart Island, although this is not always true as the weather in these regions is highly unpredictable.

The best time to take to the wilderness is usually late January through March. The weather is generally good, the kids are in school and mum and dad are back to work. If you do begin a track around Christmas, it is a good idea to start on 23 or 24 December, putting two or three days between you and the holiday crowd that is sure to follow on the better-known trails after Boxing Day; or else select a track off the beaten path. Either way you can assure yourself of a peaceful trip and a bunk in the huts.

WHAT TO TAKE

It is nice to know what the weather is going to be like, but it is better to be prepared for it. Included in every backpack should be foul weather gear such as waterproof parka and overtrousers. Many trampers carry pack covers and also wrap everything inside, especially sleeping bags and clothes, in plastic bags. To fend against the cold wind and possibly snow, you should carry along wool socks, a heavy jersey, long trousers, stocking cap and mittens. With 70 million sheep in the country or more than 20 to every person, it is little wonder that many local trampers use a considerable amount of wool in the backcountry. Actually wool has ideal properties for hikers in need of protection against New Zealand's unexpected bad weather. The bulky, fibrous make-up of wool gives it superb insulation qualities even when wet. And since the fibres themselves do not become saturated, wool is able to pull moisture off the skin while drying faster than cotton. Cotton, on the other hand, absorbs and retains water, does not hold in body heat when wet, and takes forever to dry out while hanging over a wood stove. For New Zealand tramps, wool socks, hat and mittens are a must and most trampers above the bushline will take woollen shirts and trousers. All of this, of course, delights the Kiwi sheep farmers.

Hardcore trampers have a couple of other peculiarities in their equipment lists in New Zealand, not often seen elsewhere. Many take a pair of tennis shoes to protect the life of their boots. Certain tracks, or the beginning of many, can easily be hiked in tennis shoes with no fear of foot injuries. Then upon arrival at rocky areas, steep inclines, or poor sections of the trails, trampers change into their hiking boots. The concept behind this practice is that it's a lot cheaper to replace tennis shoes then a good pair of leather hiking boots.

A lot of hiking is done in nylon shorts, Adidas running shorts being by far the most common. In the lowlands where the rain is warm and sometimes a constant occurance, nylon shorts fare much better than pants or waterproof overtrousers. The shorts may become wet but they dry quickly and if woollen socks and shirt are worn, the legs rarely get cold while actively hiking.

Also very useful for New Zealand tramping are candles, as most huts have no lighting. Gaiters to protect the boot tops and ankles are also handy. On many tracks mud, swampy sections and bog are unavoidable, and on Stewart Island gaiters are almost a necessity as the tracks are famous, or infamous, for their muddy conditions even after a week of sunshine.

If you bring tents, sleeping bags, or hiking boots into the country, it is best to have them thoroughly cleaned before departing for New Zealand. If you don't, the Agriculture Department officials will hold you up for a short spell at the airport while fumigating your dirty equipment.

Outfitting your expedition with food is easy in New Zealand. Small dairies (local grocers) carry an exceptional amount of dried and light-weight food such as cereals, vegetables, milk, soup, rice and one-pot dinners. Normally most tracks take less than a week to complete so it is not necessary to carry expensive dehydrated meals, but if your trip will be longer, and considering most trampers carry between half and one kg of food per person per day, it can pay off in the dividends of a lighter pack to invest in some meals packets. Alliance is generally considered the best brand in New Zealand and may be purchased at any camping store, but it is available only in single serving sizes and the price has risen considerably the past few years. Other brands are Vesta and Continental, which makes dinners for groups of 10 but can easily be devoured by seven or eight hungry trampers. Vesta and Continental are a little harder to find than Alliance but can usually be purchased in large supermarkets, most scout shops, or wholesale food warehouses. New Zealand also has a good supply of health food stores — one in every town it seems. They are the places to go for dried fruits, nuts, grains and other exotic items.

One last item no tramper should overlook is insect repellent. There are several kinds but Dimp is the biggest seller and most used on the tracks. Don't forget it, but don't be dismayed if it lasts only three or four hours. Like an occasional rain shower, insects and their bites are something you will just have to accept. There are mosquitoes in New Zealand but they seem pale next to the notorious sandfly.

WILDLIFE

If the kiwi ever became extinct, the sandfly could replace it as the national symbol — the little bugger is found almost everywhere. Only the high alpine areas are free from his torment. But fortunately, the sandfly has a couple of characteristics that enable trampers to survive. As long as you are moving, the sandfly won't land on you, making tramping or climbing pleasant even in the most infested areas. Sunbathing, fishing or meditating are another story. If one lands on you, it is easy to kill as quickness and alertness are not two of its strong points. But its best trait is that it usually disappears at night, allowing you a well-deserved sleep after swatting all day.

Occasionally you may venture into an area that has both mosquitoes and sandflies. Martins Bay at the end of the Hollyford Track is a classic example. Now you have a problem. The sandfly works you over during the day and the mosquito takes over at night to haunt you. In such places it might be wise to carry not only a good insect repellent but also mosquito netting to insure a sound sleep in the huts. The only thing worse than a sandfly bite during the day is a mosquito buzzing around your ear at night.

Other wildlife in New Zealand is neither as plentiful nor as tormenting. Originally, before the days of the Maoris, New Zealand had only one land mammal, a bat that came in two species. But there was a thriving bird population including the famous moa, an ostrich-like bird that grew up to heights of four metres. Today just the reverse is true. Beginning with the Maoris, who hunted the moas into extinction, and continuing with the Europeans, humans changed the wildlife scene. Rats, dogs, cats, deer, goats, possums, hares, wild pigs, ferrets, and of course sheep, were introduced into the country. Some didn't fare so well, others went on a breeding spree. Today in many of the national parks and state forests, deer and possums are so abundant that they are causing serious problems with the natural vegetation.

The native birdlife, meanwhile, suffered greatly. Rats, wild cats and dogs attacked flightless birds or ate the young and eggs of others until many of the native species have either become extinct or extremely rare. Others have survived the ordeal and among those you are bound to see are the kea or mountain parrot, the weka or wood hen, fantails which will flutter around you, and wood pigeons. The best place to study the bird life is Stewart Island where many species have survived and are strong in numbers.

The national bird, the kiwi, is also around but rather difficult to see since it is nocturnal — sleeping during the day, feeding at night — and shy by nature. But if you are willing to lose a few winks, it may be seen occasionally during night walks. Your best bet is to look in thick bush after midnight and around areas which have been overturned, since the kiwi hunts the ground for insects with his long beak. If you are intent on seeing one in the wild, check with local rangers as to where the most recent sightings have occurred. Various species of the kiwi range from Stewart Island to the Northland, but most people spare themselves that midnight search and just visit a nocturnal house at almost any zoo in New Zealand.

The one animal that was introduced and has made a hit with everyone is the trout. Before the Europeans arrived, there were virtually no freshwater fish in New Zealand. The English planted the brown trout, via Tasmania, in 1867 and in 1883 the California rainbow was imported. The country's superb water and natural environment in the lakes and streams soon lead to a thriving and massive species that easily exceed their ancestors. Today New Zealand is world renowned for its great trout fishing and it is well worth the weight to carry the proper fishing equipment on many of the tracks.

Those who want to mix tramping with fishing or hunting should make a trip to the Government Tourist Bureau where you can obtain information about seasons and regulations and buy a licence for fishing. A licence is not needed, nor is there a limit or a season, for hunting deer, elk, chamois, wild pigs or goats. A permit is required to hunt in national parks, state forests and scenic reserves and may be picked up at the headquarters of each area. There is a season for duck hunting which begins May 1 and runs for three weeks. A licence is required and may be obtained at a local outdoor or sporting goods store. Take note if you are hunting. Hunters are not supposed to use the huts in national parks that have been built for trampers. In practice, however, this is not the case and hunting parties have been known to move into a hut for extended periods.

North Island — east

Coromandel State Forest Park
Lake Waikaremoana Track
Whakatane-Waikare River Track

It's in the trees. Urewera National Park and Coromandel Peninsula share the country's common traits of rugged terrain, beautiful lakes and fast running streams. But it is the trees and the magnificent forests they make up that capture the imagination of those passing through.

The Maoris saw each tree as a living spirit while the first Europeans, with axes in their hands, quickly spotted the riches under the bark. Trampers wander through many of the same trees today and sense both — value in the wilderness solitude they offer, and mystic appeal in the Maori tales and logging relics that surround them.

Urewera, the second largest national park in the country with 210,897 hectares, is set in the rugged Urewera Range but covered from tip to toe by lush forests. There seem to be few breaks in the primeval forest, even the peaks are blanketed by mountain beech. The bush tends to overwhelm those who tramp into the area with its intense and overpowering presence. Combined with the magically rippling waters of Lake Waikaremoana and the Maori myth that lingers, it gives the national park a special aura all its own.

Coromandel State Forest Park, situated east of Thames, is a number of blocks along the peninsula that total 74,000 hectares of rugged forested hills. It is broken up by the Coromandel Range and in early times was the site of the massive kauri stands which produced a short-lived logging boom. Today there is a silent reminder of yesterday's feast as wooden dams, pack horse tracks and tram routes are left from the heyday of logging.

Originally the peninsula had a variety of rich forest flora unmatched by any other area of the country of comparable size. Now it is the site of a vigorous regrowth of kauri and forested valleys of rata, a tree noted for its brilliant orange-red flowers, and rimu. On the lower slopes are growths of matai, kahikatea and tanekaha, while on the steep ridges and high plateaus there are isolated stands of large kauri. To add to the great variety of flora are plantations of introduced pine in the Kauaeranga Valley, dwarfed trees above 600 metres and even a subalpine herbfield on Mt Moehau, the highest peak at 892 metres.

Urewera National Park also boasts of a wide variety of flora including rimu, northern rata and tawa forests in the lower reaches of the park and mountain beech on most peaks. The area around Lake Waikaremoana includes miro with its large red berries and ngutu-kaka, a rare flowering plant found in its wild state only here or great Barrier Island. Being in the upper section of the North Island, both parks are often the first introduction for many trampers to the botanical wonders of the country.

They can also be a pleasant first chapter to tramping in New Zealand. Both· are developed with well marked trails, many mild in difficulty that are ideal for hikers undertaking their first overnight expedition. Urewera also has over 50 huts for backpackers that are maintained by the National Park Board or the NZFS.

But the best tramping quality of the two parks might be their weather. Coromandel offers a mild, moist climate with long dry periods of one to three months in the summer and few frosts in the winter. Rain averages 1250 mm per year in the valleys and 2500 mm higher in the ranges. The rainfall is heavier in Urewera, 2500 mm or more, and carried into the area by north-west and southerly winds that can be particularly cold and wet in the winter. But generally the park enjoys hefty doses of sunshine in the summer and mild temperatures most of the year. Both parks have longer tramping seasons than those in the South Island and can be undertaken from November through May with the expectation of pleasant weather.

The major differences between them is Coromandel's close location to Auckland. The state forest park with its easy tracks is a favourite with Kiwis from New Zealand's largest city. On holidays or at the height of the summer, the park is well used, especially the popular Kauaeranga Valley. It is also a favourite first-time trek for many overseas visitors, wishing to ease into the country's wilderness in a relatively mild area.

Although the state forest offers only mediocre fishing and no deer herds for the hunter, wildlife abounds with a good number of native birds. Species include bellbird, tui, kokado, long-tailed cuckoo, fantails, various ducks and warblers, ring-neck pheasant, finches and the brown kiwi. The park is also noted for its tiny and rare Hochstetter's and Archey's frogs. And there are the fascinating glow-worms, easy to find after a rainfall along the banks of streams.

The park is also noted as an excellent source of gemstones and rare rocks. In or near most streams are various kinds of jaspers, petrified wood, rhodonite and agate that make the area popular with rockhounds. Permits are needed from park headquarters to collect rocks and only a geological hammer is allowed to abstract them from the environment.

Long term expeditions and huts are limited in the state forest, but there is a wide variety of overnight tramps and day hikes to choose from. Best access is the road into Kauaeranga Valley off of SH 25 at the south end of Thames. The road allows visitors deep into the park and will lead them to the NZFS headquarters. It gives access to several picnic and swimming areas along the Kauaeranga River and connects with over 50 km of tracks. The trails cover everything from leisurely nature walks to overnight tramps along the rugged mountain country beyond, where four NZFS huts are located.

Many relics of the gold and logging days are located in the valley, including a dozen dams in various degrees of decay that were used in the early 1900s.

More isolated from large urban areas, Urewera National Park does not experience the great summer influx of trampers that Coromandel State Forest does. Here the angler can find unspoiled trout fishing in the Whakatane, Waimana or Waiau rivers or sections of Lake Waikaremoana. The hunter has four species of deer to stalk and the tramper can choose from a good variety of tracks that range from a day, a week or even longer.

The main access road is SH 38 which runs from Rotorua to Wairoa and winds through the national park and around the eastern shore of Lake Waikaremoana, the park's rippling gem. Most geologists believe the lake was formed when the Waikare-Taheke River undercut the soft papa beds near Onepoto. An earth tremor then caused a natural dam in the gorge, creating the lake when water flooded the valley. Today the 55 square km of Waikaremoana are the most popular section of the national park as they offer good fishing, swimming and boating. It is also the centrepiece of the park's most scenic and heavily used track. The four or five-day walk rings the lake shore, beginning and ending near different sections of SH 38. On the eastern shores is the park headquarters at Aniwaniwa with an assortment of day hikes nearby.

The northern section of the park is the heavily forested terrain that gives Urewera its unique rugged and desolate appeal to trampers. This portion contains many challenging, long-term treks for the experienced backpacker. Included in that category is the five to six-day walk up the Whakatane River and a five-day trip up the Waimana River, starting at Maungapohatu, an important culture and historical area for the Maoris.

Colourful Maori myth is not the only thing that makes Urewera unique. The park also has some very interesting wildlife because of its vast areas of undisturbed forest. Foremost are the long and short-tail bats, the only natural mammals of New Zealand, which exist in their largest numbers in Urewera. The long-tail is extremely rare, but the short-tail can occasionally be seen or heard at night as it chases insects.

The park is also the home for two families of lizards, the green geckos and the reddish brown skink that can grow to 18 cm long. The introduced animals of pigs, goats, possum and deer are present along with the common bush birds that are found in Coromandel and other parks in the North Island.

HISTORY

From the valleys, ridges and lakes of Urewera, Maoris have been weaving their stories and tales for centuries, making the area culturally priceless. Much of the area's mystical charm and forbidding nature comes from the high spiritual value placed on it throughout history. They believed every tree possesses its own spirit and the dense forests were home for fairy folk and haunting ghosts of past ancestors. Life for the Maoris in Urewera began, so the legends say, when Hine-Pokohu-Rangi, the Mist Maiden, married a mountain and her children became the fierce tribe known as Tuhoe. Genealogical evidence points to the arrivals of the Tuhoe in 1350 when the epic Maori migration landed in the North Island. One canoe, the Mataatua, landed at the mouth of the Whakatane River and its occupants quickly moved up the hinderlands. It was a union between this tribe and the ancient Maori that already occupied sections of Urewera from which Tuhoe Potiki was born, the founder of the new tribe.

The myth might be a better explanation as the Tuhoe became a mountainous tribe which endured hardships and isolation unknown to other Maoris in New Zealand. What evolved were fierce warriors who resisted European invasion and change long after other sections of the country were settled and tamed.

The Tuhoe did not count Lake Waikaremoana as part of their lands as it was already settled by the east coast tribe, Ngati Ruapani. They held a myth that one of their ancestors, Mahu, ordered his daughter to fetch water from a spring to quench his thirst. When she refused, he went to the spring and waited until curiosity overcame her and she wandered off to find him. The father grabbed the girl and held her in the lake until she drowned. But only her body died, her spirit was turned into a taniwha (water monster) that desperately tried to escape. First she thrust north and formed the Whanganui Arm before the Huiarau Range stopped her. Then she formed the Whanganui-O-Parua Arm before attempting to escape from the lake's mouth near Onepoto. But time ran out when dawn arrived and sunlight, fatal to all taniwhas, turned her into stone. The rock can still be seen today near the outlet of the lake as well as islets that are said to be other children Mahu drowned in an angry rage.

The Tuhoe envied the Ngati Ruapani but never moved on their land until the tribe murdered two Tuhoes, one being a chief, at Hopuruahine in 1823 and desecrated the bodies. The Tuhoe warriors, lean and hard from living in the inhospitable Urewera interior, sought revenge for the act and defeated the Ngati Ruapani in a battle at the Whanganui Arm that became the beginning of a 40-year war. By 1830, however, the Tuhoe had completely dominated their opponent and taken over Waikaremoana. Peace between the two tribes was finally made in 1863 after most of the Ruapani were driven from the lake district.

Urewera was kept free from any outside influence by the Tuhoe who closely guarded their isolation and clung to a natural suspicion of Europeans. Not so of the Coromandel Peninsula. In November, 1796, Captain James Cook sailed in a rugged by on the eastern shore of the peninsula, raised the British flag over New Zealand for the first time and labeled the inlet, Mercury Bay, after spotting the planet at night.

The European invasion was lighting quick. The good stands of kauri drew the first timber ship to the Firth of Thames in 1794 and a minor logging boom followed in the early 1800s. Overseas timber traders cut as much of the good timber as their ships would hold while fires, some lasting for months, took their share of the primeaval forest. Quickly the seemingly endless hectares of trees did indeed have an end.

The timber boom, which gave rise to Thames, was followed by another boom which gave life and colour to the town that once was a rival of Auckland. In 1852, the peninsula would be known around the world as the first gold strike in New Zealand. Goldfields Reward Committee was formed in Auckland to turn the tide of young men leaving the country during the current depression for goldfields elsewhere. The committee offered a £500 reward in 1852 for the discovery of the first payable goldfield in the North Island. Charles Ring, fresh from the California fields, soon came up with a nugget from Driving Creek and rushed to Auckland to claim his reward. Thousands of miners flocked to the peninsula and Ring's goldfield to stake claims but discovered the gold was not easy pickings. The committee, meanwhile, decided it was not in payable quantities and denied Ring the reward.

The real gold rush followed others in the South Island that spurred renewed interest in Coromandel. The metal was discovered 56 km away from Thames in 1866. In the following year, the Shotover Mine was opened and produced $491,294 worth of bullion before closing in 1933. By the end of that year there were an estimated 5000 miners working the peninsula near Thames, now a bustling city. The miners came from around the world and brought with them the names of their mines — Abraham Lincoln, Belgium, Chicago, Bank of England, Just-in-Time.

Record yields were achieved in the golden years of 1869 to 1871 when the big three, the Caledonian, Golden Crown and Manukau, were in full production. Thames was also at its height of prosperity as it boasted over a hundred hotels, three theatres and a population twice that of Auckland. Today only seven of these hotels remain in a town a slice of the size of Auckland. The gold boom again spurred on the logging industry while gumdiggers soon followed, and by the turn of the century the peninsula was stripped by all who were exploiting it.

During the bustle and growth of the Coromandel, Urewera remained the dark and forbidden place it had always been. Missionaries were the first whites to explore the area when the Rev William Williams travelled through the region in November 1840 and came across Lake Waikaremoana.

But the Tuhoe resisted any intrusion by Europeans as they had little to offer them in the way of trading goods. Their first musket cost them 10 slaves in 1830. Thirty years later the tribe and the crown came into conflict at Orakau where the Tuhoe suffered a severe defeat.

They were defeated but not beaten for Tuhoe destiny took a turn in 1868. It was then that Te Kooti, the notorious Maori leader against the crown, escaped from prison on Chatham Islands and sought refuge in Ureweras. Te Kooti and the tribe formed a pact that led to a running battle with government troops for more than four years. The crown troops followed a scorched earth tactic in attempting to eliminate the Tuhoe food supplies and flush them from the woods. Te Kooti used his unique military manoeuvres to score victories over the troops and stage successful raids on towns, including Rotorua.

But the Tuhoe and their limited supplies were no match for the crown as they rentlessly stalked and hunted down Te Kooti throughout their land. Several times Te Kooti was almost captured only to have good fortune on his side. Once a premature gunshot tipped him off to the approaching troops and another time wet gun powder prevented his capture. But that proved to be the final stroke of luck for him and the final battle for the Tuhoe. By 1872 disease and starvation overtook the tribe and shattered its morale. The Tuhoe finally ended its involvement in the Lands War by agreeing to an allegiance with the government.

Te Kooti, however, never would. The rebel leader escaped once more to King Country where he lived under the protection of the Maori chief Tawhiao. He was pardoned in 1883 and in 1891 the government granted him land near Whakatane. The Tuhoe continued its distrust of the pakeha (non-Maori people) and met government surveyors and construction workers with open hostility. The tribe was finally convinced that a road through Urewera would bring trading and agricultural benefits to them but government workers still needed troops for protection as late as 1895. Although the road reached Waikaremoana from Wairoa in 1897, it was not completed until 1930.

The gold mines in Coromandel flourished until 1911 when their decline was inevitable. As manpower was drained off for WW I, one by one the great miners boarded up their shafts. Logging continued as sawmills were cutting trees from the Kauaeranga Valley as late as 1930. Many of the dams were built at the turn of the century to create sufficient force to push the kauri logs to the tidal waters. The most notable dam, Tarawaere, was built in 1925, 10 years after booms were constructed across the river to stop logs from floating further downstream.

But like the gold, gradually the logs gave way. In 1938, the valley was proclaimed a state forest and two years later small exotic pine plantations were started. Coromandel State Forest Park was set up 1971 when 65,000 hectares were reserved, including the Kauaeranga Valley, and administered by NZFS.

Pressure to mill or farm Urewera increased after the road was put through, but development was stalled by the government as the ill effects of removing the forest were already clear. Support to reserve the forest as a watershed began as early as 1925 and after WW II support grew rapidly to turn the area into a national park. This was done in 1954 and seven years later the park had reached its present size.

GETTING STARTED
Coromandel State Forest Park, being only two hours from Auckland, is for

many their first adventure into New Zealand's backcountry or often a week-end retreat. The park can be busy during the holidays and on weekends when school and scout parties frequent the area. The middle of the week, if possible, is the best time to explore the park and Christmas is unquestionably the worse.

The jumping-off spot for most trips into the park is Thames, served daily by NZRRS buses from Auckland. The city, with its turn-of-the-century Victorian buildings, is a good place to get acquainted with the golden-laden history of the area. The NZFS office on Pollen St can supply you with track information or suggestions on various treks possible.

Quick access to the park is possible at the end of either Waiotahi Rd or Karaka Rd which begin off SH 25 in the city. Near the southern city limit is the Kauaeranga Valley Rd which heads east for 20 km into the heart of the park. The park headquarters is 10 km from Thames on the valley road and is another place where you can seek out information or leave your intentions. Hitching on the Kaueranga Valley Rd is possible during the summer because of the day-use traffic heading for picnic areas or swimming holes. On the other two roads it may be touch-and-go in trying to catch a ride to the end.

Access to Urewera National Park is from SH 38, which may be slow at times for those trying to thumb their way into the park. NZRRS has a run from Rotorua to Wairoa which stops at both Ruatahuna and Aniwaniwa. The bus leaves Rotorua at 9.15 am on Mondays, Wednesdays and Fridays and reaches Aniwaniwa at 2.40 pm. On the return route it departs Wairoa on Tuesdays and Thursdays at 8.30 am.

Although the park headquarters is at Aniwaniwa and an NZFS office is at Ruatahuna, for practical purposes Rotorua or Murupara are the best places to outfit trips into the national park. There is the chief ranger's station in Rotorua (tel: Wairoa 10 004 M) and a ranger station at Murupara (tel: 641), further east on SH 38. The headquarters at Aniwaniwa has an interesting information display and track information but the centre has little else to offer the tramper preparing for a long expedition. Ruatahuna has an NZFS ranger station because part of the area and many of the huts are administered by them. The rangers are extremely knowledgeable about the tracks and have been known to even give trampers a lift occasionally out the side road to the start of the Whakatane River Track.

The Coromandel trip is a four-day walk that runs from the end of North Tararu Rd, over Table Mountain and eventually to the end of the Kauaeranga Valley Rd. It can be done from either direction but it is an easier trek up Table Mountain from east to west; the other side is considerably steeper. The trip includes a few steep climbs and walks through swamp and bog on Table Mountain. It is rated mild, however, as the tracks are well developed, marked and used during the summer.

Lake Waikaremoana in Urewera is considered a mild to medium trip as it is also a popular, near-circular walk that involves relatively level hiking along good tracks. The journey is usually a four-day walk with nights spent at Panekiri, Waiopaoa and Te Puna huts. If undertaken from Onepoto to Hopuruahine Stream, all the climbing is accomplished in the first few hours and the rest of the trip is pleasant walking.

The trip through the interior along the Whakatane and Waikare rivers is a seven-day trek that is rated strenuous and should be attempted by only experienced trampers seeking the adventure of undeveloped tracks and routes. Much of it follows river flats and gorges where there are few markings of a track and numerous crossings are required. Under normal conditions the Whakatane and the Waikare rivers can be easily forded using proper safety precautions such as poles or lines between trampers. But after heavy rains, any river or stream on the trip can flood and prevent crossings for as much as two or three days before it returns to its normal level. Crossings on the Whakatane are bridged.

Any party attempting this route should have a map and compass to assist them as well as a tent for emergency use. Most of the huts are small and a few of them, most notably Waikare Junction and Kanohirua huts, are in extremely poor conditions. Because of its difficulty, it is wise to leave your intentions at the NZFS office in Ruatahuna or one of the park ranger stations.

The trip can be done in either direction but many trampers prefer to first tackle the Whakatane River Track as it is benched for 20 km from the start and serves as a good introduction to hiking in Urewera. The route along the Waikare River from Junction Hut to Taurawharana is a two day segment that is poorly marked, if marked at all, and winds in and out of the river bed, forcing you to cross the stream up to a hundred times. The Maungapohatu Briddle Track is also poorly cut and you simply have to take your time and search for the trail in places to avoid getting detoured.

The weather can be hot and dry during the summer in either park, but especially Urewera. Conversely, both parks can be extremely wet and miserable. So take wet weather gear, as well as sun protection and sunglasses, also a few extra pairs of socks if a large number of fords are expected. On Lake Waikaremoana Track from Onepoto, it is wise to carry along drinking water on the first day as there is little available along the Panekiri Ridge.

The Urewera National Park recreation map can be used but is limited in detail. The same holds true for the Coromandel State Forest Park Recreation Guide. Series one topographical maps to obtain are N96 and N87 for the Whakatane-Waikare River Track, N105 and N96 for Lake Waikaremoana and N49 and N44 for Coromandel State Forest Park.

COROMANDEL STATE FOREST PARK

The following trip can be started from the end of Karaka Rd or Waiotahi or North Tararu Rd further north with all three tracks eventually running into each other. Trampers should allow less time for climbing Table Mountain when going from Moss Creek Hut to Waiwawa Hut than the time given below.

North Tararu Road to Waiwawa Hut

Just north of Tararu is North Tararu Rd that heads east to the edge of the Coromandel State Forest Park along the Tararu Stream. This track is the shortest trail to the divide between Kauaeranga catchment and the coastal streams, reaching it within an hour and a half from the end of the road. It is also the most scenic as the stream moves through a wide open valley with a gentle grade and passes on occasional mine tunnel, relics from the gold rush days. The other two tracks will take between two and three hours to reach the divide, though they are closer to Thames.

Cnce on the ridge, the track continues north-east until it reaches a junction with the lefthand fork heading north to Crosbies Hut and the other departing east. Within an hour the eastern track arrives at another junction with a trail that heads south off the ridge to Kauaeranga Valley Rd. From this junction, the track begins to descend towards the Waiwawa River and in a little over an hour crosses a branch of the stream to arrive at the NZFS hut.

Accommodation: Waiwawa Hut, four bunks

Time: five hours

Waiwawa Hut to Moss Creek Hut

The track departs from the hut and follows the Waiwawa River for a short spell before ascending steadily to the south-west corner of Table Mountain. In an hour, it arrives at the junction with the track that heads east in a sharp clirrb to the top of the rrountain, 836 metres up and the highest point of the trip. The other fork, which heads south, leads to the Wainora picnic area off the Kauaeranga Valley Rd.

Trampers should take their time as the climb to the top is a steep one that will demand a few rest breaks. On the mountain plateau, trampers will most likely find swampy conditions, especially after recent showers. For a better vantage point, there are short trails to spurs in the south and south-west that allow good views of the valley and the surrounding area.

The track crosses the plateau and arrives at a junction at the eastern side with one track descending quickly back to Kauaeranga River. The other heads north-west along a ridge and descends slightly to a saddle before

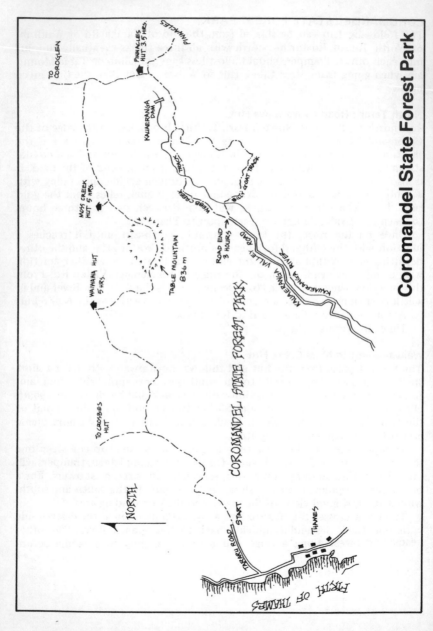

Coromandel State Forest Park

climbing again to the summit of Mt Rowe, 794 metres. The track drops off the summit and heads for Moss Creek Hut, an hour and a half from the junction and a short distance from the main track. There are a couple of old kauri dams near the hut.

Accommodation: Moss Creek Hut, 24 bunks

Time: five hours

Moss Creek Hut to Pinnacles Hut

The main track continues to head east through bush and an occasional clearing of scrub, passing still more kauri log dams. Within an hour and a half it arrives at the junction with the bulldozed track to Rangihau Rd and eventually to Coroglen. The southern fork leads off towards the Pinnacles, running alongside a power transmission line at times and eventually arriving at the Kauaeranga River, which it crosses. Down the river is the Kauaeranga Main Dam, the largest in the valley when it was built. Today only the floor and supporting stills remain. There is also good swimming in some pools near the dam.

The track resumes south by dropping slightly through scrub until it reaches a signposted junction, 45 minutes from the river crossing. Here, one fork heads south-west along with the transmission lines while the other leads off to the hut. The Pinnacles Hut is located in a depression a short distance north-east of the main track. The side trail continues past Dancing Cam Dam and in 35 minutes reaches the top of the Pinnacles.

Accommodation: Pinnacles Hut, 20 bunks

Time: three and a half hours

Pinnacles Hut to Kauaeranga Valley Road

The old bulldozed track resumes and curves to the west, passing close to the Tauranikau Dam, now just the main structural timbers. The transmission lines cross over the track and within an hour from the hut, the trail arrives at a junction. The left-hand fork follows Webb Creek to the road's end, descending the entire way and at one point using steps cut out of rock. The track crosses Webb Creek several times and eventually crosses over Kauaeranga River on a swing bridge. The road is a short distance beyond. Along the Webb Creek Track the road is two hours from the junction.

The alternative trail is Billy Goat Track, the right-hand fork that heads south and passes several dams and trestles before curving north-east to the road's end. The trail is a bulldozed track the entire way and 30 minutes or so from the road, comes to the Atautumoe Falls, a 262-metre drop of water. Billy Goat Track runs slightly longer than the trail along Webb Creek.

For those with transportation at the road's end, a day could be skipped by hiking from Moss Creek Hut all the way to the valley's floor. For those who don't, it might be best to spend a night at Pinnacles Hut and get an early start the next morning.

Time: three hours

LAKE WAIKAREMOANA TRACK

The 43-km track can be walked from either direction although by starting at Onepoto, trampers put behind them all the steep climbing the first few hours. For those walking in the opposite direction, an extra hour is needed for the tramp from Waiopaoa Hut to Panekiri and less time for the journey from Panekiri to Onepoto.

Onepoto to Panekiri Hut

The track begins at the end of the access road where the Armed Constabulary Redoubt is located. There is no time to warm up as the track immediately begins its steep climb along the yellowish sandstone cliffs of Panekiri Bluff. In three km, trampers climb from 645 metres to 1117 at the Pukenui Trig Station, one of the highest points of the trip.

At the trip station, trampers follow the track that changes from a steep climb to one that covers the ridge with all its small peaks and knobs. Most of the track still lies in beech forest on the ridge but occasionally it opens up to magnificent views of the lake, its rippling water and the various fishing vessels that look like toy boats in a bath tub. The track continues along the ridge until it confronts a sheer bluff which seems to bar the way. Closer inspection reveals a rock staircase and an aluminium ladder up the bluff where the bush has been cleared and the view improves tremendously.

After another 100 metres, the track arrives at Puketapu Trig, 1180 metres, and the Panekiri Hut right behind it. For those who sleepwalk beware! There is a sheer drop on the lake side only three metres from the the hut. Those with a big thirst should also take heed as the water supply at the hut is rainwater which can run low when the traffic is heavy during a dry spell.

Accommodation: Panekiri Hut, 18 bunks

Time: five hours

Panekiri Hut to Waiopaoa Hut

The track departs from the hut and continues to follow the ridge with its rise-and-fall-and-rise-again contour for another three km. After an hour, the track makes a sharp swing to the north where it begins its steep descent back to the lake. In less than one km, trampers lose 250 metres or much of the height they worked so hard to gain the day before.

On the way down the forest begins to change from all beech to stands of rimu and miro. Finally after one last drop over a rock slab, the track swings west, crosses a footbridge over the Waitehetehe Stream and arrives at the hut. Although it is only a three hour walk to this hut, the next one, Marauiti Hut, is another four hours and has been notorious as a hangout for mice.

Accommodation: Waiopaoa Hut, 18 bunks

Time: three hours

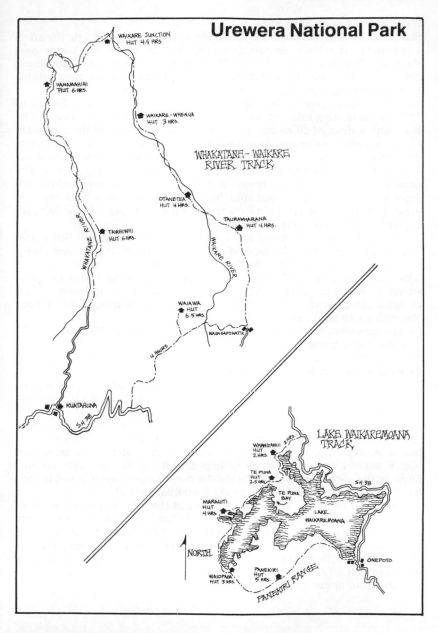

Urewera National Park

Waiopaoa Hut to Te Puna Hut

Start this day early as there are many places to linger and whittle the afternoon away. The track departs from the hut, crosses a footbridge over Waiopaoa Stream and then follows the lake shore. From here until almost the end of the trip, Lake Waikaremoana is always on the right, visible every few metres when there is a break in the thick bush.

After an hour from the hut, the track arrives at the junction to Korokoro Falls, an interesting side trip worth dropping the backpacks for awhile. The falls, with a drop of 20 metres, capitivate those who seek out the symmetry of the cascading water and its setting in the Te Korokoroowhaitiri Stream. The main track continues around the lake by climbing 50 metres above the shore before dropping to the lake again on the edge of Maraunui Bay. The track passes through a Maori reserve and its private huts before rounding the shore to the bay's end, a good spot for a dip or a cast with a favourite lure. From here the track climbs over a small saddle and then dips to Marauiti Bay and the hut, 200 metres up a side trail.

The track swings north-east and in 30 minutes from Marauiti Hut arrives at Te Kopua Bay with its white sandy beaches. It departs the bay and climbs away from the lake to cross the Te Kopua headland before returning to the lake shore. Halfway to Te Puna Hut, it passes Patekaha Island and then arrives at Waiharuru Stream where trampers must travel upstream to find an agreeable crossing. After skirting the bay, the track reaches the Te Puna Hut with its 18 bunks and open fire place.

Accommodation: Marauiti Hut, 18 bunks; Te Puna Hut, 18 bunks.

Time: seven hours

Te Puna Hut to Hopuruahine Stream

The track leaves the hut and quickly climbs up and across the neck of land that seperates the Wairau Arm from Whanganui Inlet. The walk is a pleasant one through forest but changes to mud when the track dips to the shoreline of Whanganui Inlet. An hour from the saddle, the track arrives at a grass clearing of the Whanganui Stream with the hut at its mouth. The loo at this hut is perhaps one of the most beautiful in New Zealand, strategically placed under a huge tree which is draped with orchids. Not only do they improve the view from the seat (when the door is open) when in full bloom, but the orchids must also have a strong deodorizing effect.

The track continues from the hut around the inlet where full views of the water is possible. Eventually it arrives at the Hopuruahine River which can be crossed in normal conditions with the water rising to the knees. On the other side is the access road. If the water level is too high, trampers are then forced to follow the flooded river for another 30 minutes until they reach SH 38 and its concrete bridge.

Time: four hours

WHAKATANE—WAIKARE RIVER TRACK

This trip is a seven-day trek along the Whakatane and Waikare river. For those who have less time, it is possible to hike from Tawhiwhi Hut on the Whakatane River to Waikarewhenua Hut on the Waikare River and eliminate two days of hiking, shortening the trip to five overall.

Ruatahuna to Tawhiwhi Hut

From Mataahua Turn-off to the end of the road at Waitawa Stream it is a two hour walk along the four-wheel drive vehicle track. Those with cars might want to drive only to Mataahau and walk the second half as the road becomes more broken up toward the end. There are two routes to the Tawhiwhi Hut; one, an old horse track, involves a number of river crossings and is recommended only for people with an enthusiasm for the sport, the other is a newer track which follows the true right bank of the river all the way. This is the route described here.

The track begins on a high terrace and stays in fern and bush high above the river on the eastern side and avoids the numerous fords the old horse track makes. The track stays in the edge of the hills over Te Mania Flat, crosses the Mahakirua Stream and moves through bush to climb over the rocky razorback, Horotutu. The two tracks finally come together at Ohaua Flat after the new one works through bush for a kilometre and a half to the clearing on the western shore. The new track stays on the eastern side of the river and moves through Ohaua Flat. It then crosses Manangaatiuhi Stream after climbing up a terrace. After the stream, the track climbs away from the river again to avoid swampy conditions near the shore, crosses two more flats before coming to the southern end of a third where Tawhiwhi Hut is located.

Accommodation: Tawhiwhi Hut, 20 bunks

Time: six hours

Tawhiwhi Hut to Hanamahihi Hut

The old horse track heads north, crosses Mangatawhero Stream and within 30 minutes from the hut crosses Ngaawapurua Stream. On the other side it fords the Whakatane River to the eastern shore. After moving through a flat, the track crosses the river again to Ngahiramai Flat where the NZFS hut is located, an hour from Tawhiwhi Hut. Just above the Ngahiramai Hut is a flying fox that can be used to cross the river.

The track now follows the western bank closely where it will eventually pass Tarakena Rapids, climb onto a ridge and then descend back to the river. It runs along the eastern bank for over a km to pass the Niho O Te Kiore Rapids. The track again descends to the river and fords it just above Rerehape Stream. On the western side it moves through Hanamahihi Flats past an old Wharepuni and house. The flats are rough but trampers shouldn't cross the river to the eastern side. Rather, follow the flats, cross Mangahohere Stream and swing with the track back to the western shore of the Whakatane. The track swings away once more into bush and emerges at the Hanamahihi Hut, south of the Mangahohere Stream. There are good swimming holes in the Whakatane near the NZFS hut.

The new all-weather track is an alternative route and takes an hour or two less.

Accommodation: Hanamahihi, eight bunks

Time: six hours

Hanamahihi Hut to Waikare Junction

The track first crosses a swingbridge near the hut, then moves along the east bank of the river for 300 metres before dropping through thick bush to the river bed. From here and for almost the next eight km trampers must traverse the river bed by frequently, fording back and forth from one side to the other. Care must be taken by all who attempt fords of the Whakatane. During normal conditions pole crossings are all that is needed but occasionally a rope should be used in deeper sections to ensure safety. If the river is running too high, it is possible to follow an overland route over the ridge to the east of the bridge that returns to the Whakatane at the Manaotane Stream junction.

The river winds through areas of bush, scrub and open flats. The bush is thick in the beginning but gradually opens up into large flats where the river curves from the north to the west. Two hours from the hut, the route arrives at the Manaotane Stream junction where a bridle track is situated. Occasionally sections of it can be used along the southern banks. Eventually the track arrives at a flying fox which can be used to cross the Whakatane to the hut on the north bank.

Again, the all-weather track is an alternative for trampers who prefer a more straightforward route.

Accommodation: Waikare Junction Hut, six bunks

Time: 4½ hours

Waikare Junction to Otanetea Hut

One track leaves the hut and heads north along the Whakatane but trampers should backtrack over the flying fox and follow the southern bank to the Waikare River junction. Here and for the next 2½ km, the Waikare winds through a deep rocky gorge with the bush coming right down to the water's edge. There is no real track: rather, if the conditions of the river are normal, trampers should criss-cross the stream when necessary and often before reaching Waikarewhenua Hut. A few narrow gorges are the only barriers and they can be by-passed quite easily. The river is one of the most beautiful in the park but if it is swollen, and it may be for days at a time, trampers must wait it out or change their trip.

At the Otapupia Stream junction, a track resumes and begins working across river flats for the next five km, fording the river only a couple of times. Towards the southern end of the flats, across from the junction of the Motumuka Stream, the NZFS hut is located, an ideal place for afternoon tea.

A rough track leads over a terrace from the hut on the east bank of the river for a short distance. From here, trampers again make their own way along the river, crossing it when necessary. The valley begins to close again at the Opamako Stream junction and a rocky bluff appears one km below this. The bluff can be passed on either side. Okirara Stream junction is reached next and in less than one km Otanetea Hut appears on the west bank of the Waikare.

Accommodation: Otanetea Hut, six bunks

Time: seven hours

Otanetea Hut to Taurauharana Hut

The route continues along the Waikare River and in a short distance from the hut passes the Maukuroa Stream where just upstream is an impressive waterfall worth searching for. The route continues, criss-crossing the river frequently and passing the junctions of the Motuhouhi Stream to the west and Hanehane Stream to the east shortly afterwards.

The route continues along the river and eventually arrives at the old clearing of the Neketuri settlement where there is a footbridge across the Waikare. The route passes the clearing, crosses the river and finally ascends to the Taurawharana kainga where the NZFS is situated.

Accommodation: Taurawharana Hut, six bunks

Time: four hours

Taurawharana Hut to Waiawa Hut

Descend from Taurawharana to the junction of Waikare and Manakino streams where an old briddle track is located. The track ascends through bush to a ridge and follows it south. At a dip in the ridge, it arrives at the junction with the Six-Foot Track and then continues where it climbs to the peak of Tauaki, 793 metres. The track descends from the peak to the Waipaepae Stream and it crosses it to Pinaki, an old kainga. Grassy slopes here make for excellent camping but Pinaki is privately-owned and permission to camp should be sought from the farmer.

The track continues to descend, enters fern and scrub and at one point before crossing Omarana Stream, passes old Miki's corrugated iron house. Follow an old bulldozed road up the ridge on the true left bank of the Waikare. The track climbs to a saddle overlooking the Kakewahine valley. The old road continues down toward the valley floor and joins an old horse track which continues to the hut. The hut is small but in good shape with an open fireplace.

Accommodation: Waiawa Hut, six bunks

Time: 6½ hours

Waiawa Hut to SH 38

Backtrack to the main track at Kakewahine and continue to the south. The track climbs one small saddle where it fords Taurekarekarua Stream and then descends all the way to Kanohirua Hut on the south bank of the Kanohiru Stream. The hut has six bunks and has recently been renovated.

From Kanohirua it is an easier walk to SH 38 as the track first follows the Kanohirua Stream and then takes swing to the south. Here it hugs the east bank of Mahakirua Stream, crosses over to the other side at the junction with Ahimate Stream and follows the west bank of the latter to SH 38, ending at Papatotara Ridge, 792 metres.

Time: four hours

North Island — west

Mt Egmont Round-The-Mountain Track

First it tantalized the Maoris who made it a god. Then it fascinated Captain Cook on the deck of the *Endeavour* in 1770. Today thousands make the pilgrimage to the summit of Mt Egmont, the lonely volcano that accents the Taranaki region of the North Island.

The near perfect symmetry of its cone makes Mt Egmont a twin to Japan's Mt Fuji and one of the most beautiful mountains in New Zealand. The easy accessibility to tracks and its magnificent views of patchwork dairyland, stormy Tasman Sea or rugged Tongariro peaks make it a favourite with trampers.

Mt Egmont's present shape comes from a series of eruptions that occurred 16,000 years ago and gave the cone its smooth lines and eye-pleasing beauty. The only flaw in the mountain is made by Fantham's Peak, the cone on the south slope of the volcano. Snow-capped on a clear winter day, Egmont is surely one of the country's most stunning sights, unmatched by any individual mountain in the southern Alps.

The entire mountain along with the Kaitake and Pouakai Ranges, a line of volcano activity, lies in the Egmont National Park. The preserved wilderness includes 33,532 hectares of native forest and bush, 320 km of tracks and routes and 17 park board huts and shelters scattered throughout the area. Three roads serve as main routes of access to the area and allow motorists to drive up to the 900-metre level or close to the bushline of the mountain.

The roads allow inexperienced trampers to scale the summit, an easy ascent from Dawson Falls or the Plateau during good weather in the summer. The road encourages families, school classes and novice trampers to tackle a number of day tracks or overnight routes. At the end are also motel, lodge and restaurant accommodation at Statford Mountain House and Dawson Falls and a large bunkhouse at North Egmont. All of this stimulates a heavy use of the park by both experienced trampers and day hikers during the Christmas period and into the height of the summer. In the winter, Mt Egmont becomes the second major ski area in the North Island.

But away from the heavily used regions, trampers will find their solitude and backcountry peace of mind as the rest of the park experiences only a moderate number of hikers that is easy to contend with. The spectacular

41

views above the bushline and the unique forests and vegetation below will be worth any number of trampers passed on the tracks.

The circular boundary of the park lies at the altitude of 360 metres while the summit of Mt Egmont is 2517 metres. In between, covering all sides of the cone, are gorges and valleys carved out by streams and resulting in some majestic waterfalls, particularly Dawson Falls with its drop of 18 metres and Bell Falls with its drop of 31 metres. But Egmont's hidden value is the way the area absorbs and retains a vast proportion of the province's generous rainfall, exceeding 8000 mm some years on the upper slopes. In this aspect, the mountain holds an important role in the development and prosperity of the region as a dairy and farming province.

Mt Egmont displays the maritime climate with a moderate change in seasons that most of the country experiences. The average temperature in the warmest month, February, is 18°C and dips to 10°C in the coldest, July. The air temperature decreases 6°C for every 1000 metres you climb, making the freezing level at 3500 metres in the summer and 1750 metres in the winter. Snow is rare in the summer months but thin sheets of ice on rocks and other bare surfaces are not when temperatures drop suddenly in the upper alpine sections.

The park does have some characteristics of its own when it comes to weather. Egmont and the surrounding mountains force the moist air of the Tasman sea to rise, cool and then condense into rain, hail or snow. The mean annual rainfall for the North Taranaki coast is 1500 mm, but at the 1000 metre level of Egmont it is 6500 mm and at the 2000-metre level it is a soaking 8000 mm. The high rainfall and the absence of long dry spells produces the growth of dense vegetation that once covered the entire Taranaki region, now preserved only in the park.

Not only does Egmont cause more rain but its altitude creates greater exposure to wind and temperatures. This leads to a rapid and unexpected arrival of bad weather or even squall and storm conditions at high altitudes. Throw together strong winds, possible freezing temperatures at night, and early morning fog that sharply reduces visibility, and you have alpine dangers that have taken over 40 lives. With Egmont, as with the rest of New Zealand's alpine regions, you need to be fully prepared for any kind of weather.

The bush and flora of Egmont also set it apart. Those familiar with the country's native trees will notice the complete absence of beech as well as about 100 other common mountain species. Egmont's isolation from the rest of the mountainous areas of New Zealand has lead to its unique vegetation, and the great extremes in rainfall have lead to a wide variety in its flora. A small part of the park is covered with a thick, well-shaded woodland of rimu and northern rata. The trees, which can grow to 27 metres, appear stacked behind one another, almost touching. The far more common bush is the smaller kamahi and mahoe, mixed in with stands of wineberry, broadleaf, fuchsia and pate. The rainfall and mild climate have resulted in

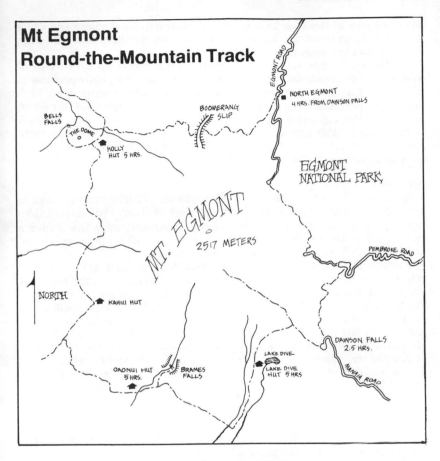

about nine-tenths of the park being covered by dense, lush forest when even on a sunny day, it seems dark and cool under its thick canopy.

Species comlonly found elsewhere in New Zealand, including tussock grass, mountain daisy, harebell, koromiko and ourisia, have developed slight distinctions on isolated Egmont. From about 1600 down to 1370 metres, trampers mostly find tussock and herbfields, accented by mountain daisies or giant buttercups. Above 1600 metres to the summit there is little plant lie while below, hardy shrubs begin to appear, notably leatherwood.

The fringes of the forest appear at 1070 metres where the average temperature has increased and the wind isn't as strong. First it is mountain cedar (kaikawaka) mixed in with leatherwood. At 900 metres kamahi, the dominant tree of the area, appears with its distinctive leaf colour and white flowers. Gradually on the lower slopes rimu and northern rata take over, towering over the kamahi.

Mt Egmont's wide variety of distinctive flora makes up for its lack of wildlife. There are no deer in the park but there are goats and opossums to the extent that their numbers are a problem for park management. Each year costly programmes of noxious animal control are carried out to prevent ravages on the vegetation by these species. Mt Egmont has the usual bush birds but its birdlife appears shallow when compared to areas of the South Island or Stewart Island. There are numerous streams and many of them offer good rewards to the persistent fisherman.

HISTORY

Volcano activity began building Mt Egmont some 70,000 years ago and in about 30,000 years resulted in a good size cone of about 1500 metres. Geologists believe the mountain then entered a dormant stage that ended a mere 3000 years ago with a series of eruptions. When they were over, Egmont was left with its near perfect cone of today.

Activity continued with the Newall Eruptions in 1500 AD, which destroyed much of the surrounding bush with gas-charged clouds, and the latest known eruptions in 1755, only 15 years before Cook sighted the mountain. There is a question among geologists today whether Mt Egmont is still active or not. Some point to dormant periods that lasted several thousand years and say the last eruption was too recent to be sure. Others believe its days of lava and streaming ash are over and gradually, with natural erosion of rain and ice, Egmont will wear down as have Kaitake and Pouakai.

The Maoris had a different view of the volcano. They believed Egmont, known to them as Taranaki, originally lived among the central mountains of the North Island. One day Taranaki captured the heart of Tongariro's wife, Mt Pihanga, while her husband was away. Tongariro was enraged when he returned and caught the pair of lovers by surprise. In the mountainous struggle that followed, Taranaki was exiled from the range. The volcano retreated west, carving out the Wanganui River Valley, and formed the Te Ngaere Swamp while resting near Stratford. Finally he settled on the coast.

Taranaki still gazes at his true love and today when there is a mist surrounding the peak, he is said to be weeping. Pihanga will still a sigh occasionally in smoke when thinking of her lost one, while Tongariro, the enraged husband, fumed in anger for years.

To the Maoris, Egmont was sacred, a place where the bones of chiefs were buried, a hideout to escape the terrorism of other tribes. The legendary Tahurangi was said to be the first person to climb to the summit where he lit a fire to claim the surrounding land for his tribe. The Maoris lived around the base until the Waikato invaders massacred the inhabitants, despite their secret caves, in the 1820s and 30s with muskets. The survivors fled the area and headed south, leaving only a handful remaining on the rocky Sugar Loaf Islands.

The first European to see Mt Egmont was Cook in 1770 who along with his crew was so impressed that one shipmate wrote later it was 'the noblest hill I have ever seen'. Cook named the mountain in honour of Earl Egmont, first lord of the Admiralty. Dutch explorer Abel Tasman was actually the first European to sail past the mountain in 1642 but the cone was shrouded in clouds, and was passed by unnoticed. Two years after Cook, Mt Egmont was the first thing French explorer Marion du Fresne saw of New Zealand. He thought it was an islet until he noticed snow on top of the cone.

Both Cook and du Fresne recorded seeing fires of Maori settlers but never made contact with them. Naturalist Ernest Dieffenback did, however, in 1839. Working for the New Zealand Company, he told the local Maoris of his plans to climb to the summit. The Maoris tried passionately to dissuade him from his ascent but Dieffenback set out for the top anyway. Although this attempt was unsuccessful, the naturalist set out again a year later and this time reached the peak. The Maori guides, however, left him at the snowline as the upper slopes were 'tapu' to them.

By boiling water and using thermometers, Dieffenback placed the height of the mountain at 2694 metres. In 1850, a trigonometrical survey of the peak was performed by the crew aboard *HMS Acheron*, anchored in New Plymouth. They placed the height at 2520 metres and it wasn't until 110 years later in 1960 when a theodolite was carried to the summit that the present height was determined at 2517 metres.

Like its sister park, Tongariro, Egmont quickly became a haven for trampers and adventurers. The area was temporarily reserved under a provision in the Lands Claim Act of 1877 after hiking parties to the summit by way of the Pouakai Range and New Plymouth became a regular activity in the summer. The act was made permanent two months later and included the peak and a six-mile radius around it.

In 1885 Thomas Dawson discovered the falls that now bear his name and later was influential in the development of a track and campground in the area of the Dawson Falls Tourist Lodge.

The first woman to scale the slopes of Panitahi was Fanny Fantham in 1887 and the parasite cone on the south side of Egmont was renamed in her honour. Along with Fantham's Peak, Lake Dive was also named after a member of the expedition, Bradshaw Dive.

A route to the summit from Straford Plateau and the development of the area took place in 1888, while in 1901 H M Skeet completed the monumental task of surveying the area for the first topographical map. After that, development increased at a feverish pace with the construction of huts, access roads and additional tracks around the mountain.

The national park emerged in October 1900 when an act of government set up the first park board. Later an area of 33,500 hectares of the Kaitake Range was added to the park.

GETTING STARTED

New Plymouth, the coastal city with Mt Egmont as a backdrop, is the jumping off spot for most hikers arriving in the area. The city, a six-hour drive from Auckland, has every supply needed to outfit an extended trek around the mountain, and is the location of a Lands and Survey department office where valuable information can be obtained. There is also a ranger station located on Pembroke Rd in Stratford, and a park display centre at Dawson Falls at the end of Manaia Rd.

There are over 30 roads that lead to or near the park and most of them have a track from the roadhead. Three of them, Egmont, Pembroke and Manaia Rds, take you to 900 metres up the mountain and close to the bushline. They are the most common means of access to the park as they lead to accommodation facilities and information boards about the area and the tracks in their vicinity.

For hiking the Round-the-Mountain Track, Egmont is the best road to take as it is the closest to New Plymouth and does not have the busy and often hectic motel/hotel trade that the other two do. If driving, you can leave your car at the end and it will be a welcome sight when you complete the circular track. If backpacking, you can catch a bus from either New Plymouth or Stratford to Egmont Village, the junction to the park, and then hitchhike to the end of Egmont Rd. During the late spring and throughout summer it is fairly easy to catch a ride to the trailhead. It is also possible for those with a hiking party of several to hire a Newman's minibus up the road as Newman's run daily tours of Mt Egmont.

First night accommodation for many at North Egmont is the Camphouse that provides bunkroom style quarters for 32. Inquiries should be made at the North Egmont Visitor Centre. At Dawson Falls there is a park board hut that sleeps 38 as well as motel accommodation. The North Egmont Chalet, mentioned in many old travel guides and maps, is no longer in operation.

The most popular hike in the park is the climb to the summit, an adventure that is accomplished by trampers of all ages during the summer. People with little tramping experience can reach the summit as part of an open climb, arranged by local alpine clubs and led by experienced guides. These are usually held in late January or early February. Inquire at the New Plymouth public relations office for details.

The variety of day walks and overnight tramps are too numerous to list but there is one of every length and difficulty to fulfil any tramper's desire. Longtime favourites for day hikes are Bell Falls, Dawson Falls, Enchanted Walk or the Mangaoraka Track off the Egmont Rd.

The trip described in this chapter is a four-day tramp around Mt Egmont, beginning and ending at North Egmont. The track is rated medium and can be undertaken by trampers new to the ways of the wilderness if they are prepared with the right equipment and the proper knowledge. The longest single day's hike is the final one from Lake Dive back to North Egmont, taking most hikers from six to seven hours. An extra day should be included if you are interested in scaling Egmont's peak.

All trampers, both novice and experienced, should be aware of Egmont's dangers before embarking on a trek. The mountain often holds a false appearance of being an easy hike. This and the high altitude access put inexperienced people within reach of steep icy slopes with conditions combining to take the lives of unprepared hikers. Weather on Egmont, like other alpine areas only slightly worse, can change suddenly into stormy conditions with rapidly dropping temperatures. Make sure you take warm clothing, preferably woollies, to avoid the dangers of exposure.

Trampers should also be aware of loose stone and falling rock and the dangers of sliding down frozen slopes in the alpine areas. Glissading should be done only in areas that are known to be safe. Best precaution is to sign the intentions book at every hut for a safe return.

There is a recreation map to the park; series one topographical maps N118 and N119 cover the area in finer detail.

TRACK DESCRIPTION
Although this trip is described from North Egmont west around the cone, it can be done in either direction and from any of the three major access points.

North Egmont to Holly Hut
The track begins on the south side of the Camphouse and climbs steadily up a spur, past the Tahurangi trig station and up on Razorback Ridge. It follows the ridge past a noticeable slip and then turns west, climbing round the heads of the Ram and Waiwhakaiho Stream and along the base of Dieffenback Cliffs near the bushline. The track proceeds past a branch of the Kokowai Stream and climbs again on the Boomerang Slip, named for its unusual shape above the gorge. Gradually it ascends another ridge and comes to the junction with Kokowai Track. Kokowai is the Maori name for red ochre, or iron carbonate, the main element of their paint for buildings and carvings. Much of it can be seen around the area and down the Kokowai Gorge.

After crossing a few ridges and streams, the track descends towards the Ahukawakawa Swamp and arrives at the junction with the Ahukawakawa Track. The left fork crosses two branches of the Minarapa Stream before reaching Holly Hut. From the hut it is another two km or a 30 minute walk around the Dome to Bell Falls, a spectacular sight of water cascading down a 31-metre cliff.

Accommodation: Holly Hut, 26 bunks
Time: three hours

Holly Hut to Oaonui Hut
A good track leads west from Holly Hut to Bell Falls junction a few

hundred metres away. The left-hand fork, Round-The-Mountain Track, then descends a clay face below Hook Hill and crosses Peters Stream. The stream is named after Harry Peters, well-known guide and Camphouse caretaker at North Egmont in the 1800s and '90s.

From Peters Stream to Kahui Hut, the track wanders through scrub and mossy slopes, a result of a landslide 100 years ago that lowered the bushline. The track continues after Peters Stream around the lower slopes of Skinner Hill and then climbs slightly to the deeply eroded Pyramid Stream. It crosses three major arms of the stream, gradually descends back across moss slopes and into scrub at Maero Stream. Shortly after crossing the stream, the track comes to the junction with Puniho Track. The left-hand fork continues through scrub and 30 minutes from Maero Stream, reaches Kahui Hut, a good place for lunch.

Follow the Kahui Track, a well developed trail, as it leaves the hut and slowly descends into dense bush again. After half an hour the Kahui track joins the Oaonui track. Take this left-hand fork which shortly crosses branches of the Okahu Stream and then continues south around the mountain through bush for an hour. The track crosses two branches of the Oaonui Stream; the hut is located on the far side of the second branch.

Accommodation: Oaonui Hut, four bunks

Time: five hours

Oanui Hut to Lake Dive

The Brames Falls Track continues east around the mountain from behind the hut and quickly crosses a dry stream bed by an aluminium bridge. It then descends a ladder on the west side of the Waiaua River and into the steep gorge created by the stream. After crossing the stream and climbing out, the track turns northward and follows the west bank of the gorge. It ascends slightly to the junction with the Taungatara Track, an hour or four km from Oaonui Hut. The right-hand fork leads off to the Lake Dive Track. But for those who have time and energy, there is a good view of Brames Falls half a km further up the left-hand fork. A hike to the scenic falls is a two-hour return trip from Oaonui Hut that follows the gorge most of the way.

The Taungatara Track cuts south-east around Egmont to the Lake Dive Track by descending slightly as it crosses three major streams before arriving at the junction with the Mangahume Track which joins from the south. The Taungatara Track dips down a gorge and crosses the Mangahume Stream and later the Taungatara Stream by means of a natural bridge. After a few more streams and a four-hour tramp from the Oaonui Hut, the Taungatara Track joins Lake Dive Track on the east side of the Punehu Stream.

The Lake Dive Track heads north following the Punehu Stream and after a while runs along the eastern bank of the gorge the stream created. After passing the two Beehive Hills on the right, the track opens up to the lake and the hut on the eastern shore, both in the shadow of Upper Beehive Hill,

height 952 metres.
   Accommodation: Lake Dive Hut, 16 bunks
   Time: five hours

Lake Dive to North Egmont

The track to Dawson Falls leaves the Lake Dive hut and climbs steadily towards Fanthams Peak. After about 30 minutes' hiking, the track begins to leave the dense, heavy bush and comes into alpine scrubland and then moss-covered slopes, climbing steadily until it reaches the Summit Track above Kapuni Lodge. For those who wish to include a trek to the summit, this would be the best opportunity. The left-hand fork is the summit route and leads past Fanthams Peak to the top of Mt Egmont. It is not a track, but a route marked by poles, tags and rock Cairns and should be attempted only during fair weather. It is a three or four-hour tramp to the peak from the junction and most likely an extra day would be needed to undertake it. The Park Hut at Dawson Falls which holds 38, would be suitable accommodation for an extra night.

A memorable experience for many is to hike above Lake Dive to the bushline in the first hour or two of morning or even during sunrise. The early morning light on the eastern slopes of Egmont on a clear day is a dramatic scene, well worth putting off breakfast for an hour or two.

For those continuing on to North Egmont, take the right-hand fork which heads east and quickly descends past the side track to Kapuni Lodge. From there it is another km to Hooker Hut, a day use shelter with no bunks, and then a rapid descent to the clearing right above the display centre at Dawson Falls. The centre, run by the Lands and Survey Department, is well worth a visit.

From Dawson Falls, the trail resumes at the tourist lodge and climbs past Victoria Falls and Wilkies Pools, an interesting pool created by the Kapuni Stream flowing into a lava outcrop. There is also Twin Falls and Bubbling Springs nearby with short side tracks leading to them. The track then ascends to the junction with the Ridge Trail and finally to The Plateau, and then turns into a four-wheel-drive road to the Manganui Gorge. Here the walking track resumes and goes down, up and out of the rugged gully and past a public shelter and the Manganui Ski Lodge.

From the ski lodge it is a gentle climb to Tahurangi Lodge, passing along the way the junction to the Waipuku Track and hut on the east and Hen and Chickens Spur on the west. At the Tahurangi Club Lodge the track joins Translator Rd which passes down Puffer Ridge, descends into Ngatoro Valley and finally climbs the remaining 200 metres to North Egmont.
   Time: 6½ hours

North Island — central

Tongariro Round-The-Mountain Track
Kaimanawa State Forest Park

In a country noted for its contrast, Tongariro National Park offers the most. Its trademark is volcanoes and three of them — Ruapehu, Ngauruhoe and Tongariro — form the park's impressive skyline. But it stretches from stands of giant red beech and rimu to tussock grasslands and alpine gravelfields to the only desert in New Zealand. In the summer, Kiwis are scrambling up its peaks, in the winter they are skiing down. It can be the busy Chateau Tongariro bustling with people and life or nearby Kaimanawa State Forest Park where there are few traces of humanity in the deep beech forests. It can be well benched trails or barely cut tracks. It can be almost anything.

And to the Maoris, it was. For centuries the thermal activity and volcanoes were a sacred area. Today it still inspires thousands to spend their holidays at the country's first national park. The area is the southern end of a volcanic chain that extends north-west through the heart of the North Island past Taupo, Ohaki, Rotorua and finally White Island. The thermal phenomenon begins across the Pacific Ocean, thousands of km from New Zealand, and is responsible for Tongariro's hot springs, boiling mud pools, fumeroles and the maze of craters scattered throughout the park as well as the volcanoes.

But the three volcanoes attract the most attention. At 2796 metres, Ruapehu is the tallest mountain in the North Island and its snowfields and glaciers provide the best runs for skiers. It also holds Crater Lake, a body of warm, acid water surrounded by ice and snow. The lake froze over in 1926 and was replaced by a lava dome in 1945. Next to Ruapehu is Ngauruhoe, a nearly perfect symmetrical cone of 2291 metres and the most continually active volcano in the mainland. Mt Tongariro at 1968 metres is the smallest and the northernmost of the three.

The entire park contains 76,198 hectares and since its formation in 1887 has been well developed for recreational use. There is everything from the famous Chateau Hotel and a golf course to the various ski fields and a large number of tracks and day trails around the three peaks. Although a long-term trek cannot be separated from the rest of the commercial ventures, most trampers view that as a small price to pay for the outstanding features of the park. Along with great variation in the flora, the area offers exceptionally close encounters with its thermal activity, hot springs to relax weary muscles, peaks to climb and tracks that wind around the park above the bushline for extraordinary views. Most of the tracks lie in tussock grassland above the beech forests, making Tongariro the best alpine tramping in the North Island.

The Round-The-Mountain Track provides a comprehensive view of the park and of most of the 500 or so species of native plants. Trees include mountain beech, rimu, totara and matai. On the Ohakune Mountain Rd you pass rimus 30 metres tall and more than 600 years old. Here too are many of the 36 species of orchid and 60 species of fern found in the park. Below 1200 metres there are widespread red tussock areas and above 1300 metres the alpine herbfields begin and are the home of such plants as the mountain inaka, parahebes and two species of mountain buttercup.

Tongariro National Park is also the home of the Rangipo desert, a barren landscape characterised by large patches of dark reddish sand and ash with small upstanding clumps of tussock. This unique landscape is the result of the volcanic eruptions of the past two million years, especially the Taupo eruption of about 2000 years ago which coated a wide area with thick deposits of pumice, destroying all vegetation. Today the area is in a rain shadow as the prevailing westerlies shed their burden of rain and snow on Ruapehu leaving only drying winds to cut across the plain.

This barren area is the source of the Tongariro River which flows into Lake Taupo, becoming one of the most famous trout fisheries in the world. Many pools with good fishing are signposted off SH 1.

Most of Tongariro National Park lies in a mountain environment with its own unpredictable weather patterns. The western slopes of all three volcanoes are exposed to sudden adverse weather and heavy rain or even snow in early summer on the peaks. At the Chateau rain occurs on average 191 days of the year for an average of 2743 mm.

East of Tongariro National Park is Kaimanawa Forest Park, a reserve of more than 76,000 hectares characterised by its broken terrain of mountain beech, tussock and alpine scrub.

What Tongariro is, Kaimanawa isn't. One is well known, well used and has easy access; the other is half hidden from the tramper in both exposure and the lack of public transport serving it. Together, however, the two parks along with the Pihanga Rserves have provided Kiwis with a utopia for outdoor recreation that is ideally located among the North Island urban areas. Consideration is being given to preserving another large section west of Lake Taupo that would complete the preservation of the entire inland plateau for all who find peace and strength in the back country.

Kaimanawa can be divided into two general sections. The south-central part is mostly upland moors, alpine tussock and peaks that are a challenge to most trampers. The north-west is less broken and bushclad in mountain and red droves of hunters. The state park is well known for its good stocks of red and sika deer and thus its excellent hunting. NZFS rangers report that of the 10,000 users of the area every year, only 25% of them are trampers, the rest hunters.

Hunting has always been the major attraction in Kaimanawa and a much lesser one at Tongariro National Park. At the turn of the century both red and sika deer were introduced in the area and they spread rapidly, destroying the native vegetation. The government's program of deer control was so effective from the 1930s to 1950s, that today the populations can be controlled easily by private hunters. Although the red deer is fewer in number, the sika is more prized by hunters because of its elusiveness and difficulty to hunt.

Other introduced animals include wild pigs, goats, opossum and hares. All the introduced species have caused severe damage to the bird life as well as the native flora. Still, you will encounter a variety of birds throughout the region, most notably parakeets, robins and kakas.

In Kaimanawa Forest Park, most of the bush is beech with podocarps in the northern valleys. In the north-west, the forest is mostly large red beech with much already harvested by loggers, while the southern region is predominantly mountain beech. Tussock grasslands occur in the highlands and also in lowlands where Maori or European fires had burned away the forest. In the alpine regions, you find the usual snowgrass, heath-like vegetation and red tussock.

The weather is generally good in Kaimanawa with mild temperatures and sunny skies most of December through April. In the southern mountainous sections of the park, the weather can be unpredictable with heavy rain, sleet or even snow developing quickly in high altitudes during early or late summer.

HISTORY

Geologically speaking, the Tongariro volcanoes are relatively young, formed 2½ million years ago during eruptions of lava and scoria. Mt Ruapehu and Mt Tongariro were completed by the Ice Age and since have been carved to their present shape by erosion and explosions of other eruptions. Glaciers at one time extended down Mt Ruapehu below 1300 metres and have left footprints of polished rock far below their present snouts.

Mt Ngauruhoe is even younger as it was formed in an old crater of Mt Tongariro and built its near perfect cone almost 700 metres higher than the old volcano. Today it is the most active volcano in New Zealand as it tosses steam and dark clouds of ash every few years. All three, however, have a long history of fiery eruptions.

One eruption of Mt Ruapehu began in March 1945 and continued for almost a year, spreading lava above the surface of Crater Lake and sending huge dark clouds of ash as far away as Wellington. Mt Ruapehu was felt rumbling again in 1969 and 1973 but by far the worst disruption it caused was not the result of an eruption. On Christmas Eve 1953 an ice wall that held back a section of Crater Lake collapsed. An enormous mud and water flow swept down the mountainside and took everything in its path including a railway bridge. Moments later a crowded Christmas Eve train plunged into the gorge and sent 151 people to their death in one of the country's worst disasters. A year later, Mt Ngauruhoe's staged a major eruption that lasted 11 months and disgorged six million cubic metres of lava. In 1975 a brief, one-day burst sent ash 14,000 metres into the sky.

To the Maoris, the three volcanoes were 'tapu' and they sought to prevent anybody from climbing them. They believed Ngatoroirangi, high priest of the Tuwharetoa tribe of Lake Taupo, arrived in the Bay of Plenty in the Arawa canoe and travelled south to claim the volcanic plateau for his people. He told his followers to stay behind and fast until he returned and then set off with a female slave to light a fire on Mt Tongariro's summit. His followers offended the gods, however, by giving up the fast and were killed when the spirits sent down a fierce snow storm. The high priest, on the slopes of the volcano, cried out to the gods to send him warmth. To prove his devotion, he sacrificed the slave. The gods responded by sending fire from underneath that burst open throughout the North Island including the craters of Mt Ngauruhoe and Mt Tongariro. Ngatoroirangi climbed to the newly formed crater, tossed the body in and laid claim to the surrounding land for his people.

The volcanoes, especially Mt Tongariro, have been sacred to the Maoris ever since. They often travelled to Ketetahi Hot Springs to bathe but were forbidden to go any further. Europeans were also discouraged from the area and it was John Carne Bidwill, a botanist and explorer, who became the first to scale Mt Ngauruhoe in 1839. While staring into the crater, Bidwill felt the volcano rumble and watched steam drift out. This frightened the explorer and even more Te Heuheu Tukino II, the Maori chief who tried to dissuade Bidwill. For the next 12 years the local tribe was successful in keeping all away from its sacred grounds. But in 1851, Mt Ruapehu fell to a climber's passion when Sir George Grey ascended one of the volcano's peaks and then hid from his Maori guides to avoid their discontent. In 1879, George Beetham became the first to scale Mt Ruapehu and see Crater Lake and by the 1880s the Maoris could no longer deter the steady flow of geologists, explorers and botanists who were intrigued by the area.

Nor could the Tuwharetoa clan keep other Maori tribes from claiming the land. After the Land Wars, where Tuwharetoa chief Te Heu Heu IV Horonuku aided rebel Te Kooti, the tribes loyal to the Crown, or pakehas, wanted the area redistributed. In 1886, at a schoolhouse in Taupo, the Maori Land Court met to determine the ownership of land around Taupo. Many chiefs regarded Tuwharetoa land as rebel country and thus were eager to gain ownership of it for supporting the Queen.

Horonuka showed great concern and pleaded passionately to the court to leave the area intact. To him, the volcanoes were religious and he did not cherish the thought of having them split up among pakehas, who saw only grazing value in the tussock grasslands. Horonuku had often thought of selling the land to the Crown and was convinced by his son-in-law that was the only solution to its preservation. But when he discussed it with his people, it was decided to give it away not to sell.

Before the Native Land Court on 23 September 1887, Horonuku presented the area to the Crown for the purpose of a national park and made only two requests: that he be allowed to remove the remains of his father and that his son be appointed as a trustee on the administered body of the park. The move restored Horonuku's prestige in the eyes of the Maoris while today he is looked on as a rare individual with the insight on the priceless value of Tongariro's beauty over that of grazing land.

An act of Parliament created the country's first national park in 1894 but its development was slwo. Inaccessibility kept most Kiwis away from the area even though the Desert Rd was completed in the same year from Wairoru to Tokaanu. The first commercial adventure in the area was Allen Brothers Summer Camp where for 25 shillings a day one would get a guide, horse, meals and a bed at the wilderness resort near Desert Rd. An advertisement in 1895 for the camp promised 'plain but comfortable accommodations'.

The main trunk railroad reached the region in 1908 and encouraged more visitors to the area. By then there were huts at Waihohonu in the east with a track leading to them and to the hot springs at Ketetahi. The railroad brought a large number of visitors to the western side and by 1918 a track and hut were built in the Mangatepopo for skiers on Mt Ngauruhoe. A road was built to the Chateau in 1920 and within three years the Ruapehu Ski Club was already established and had a hut at the 1768-metre level on the Whakapapa slopes. The road to Top-O-The-Bruce soon followed.

The park mushroomed in the 1950s and '60s as roads were sealed, huts built and more tracks developed. In 1963, the Ohakune Mountain Rd was finished, matching the height reached by Bruce Rd and by the early 1970s, almost 400,000 visitors were enjoying the park each year.

Unlike Tongariro, Kaimanawa Forest Park is geologically very old. The Kaimanawa range is composed of a steel-blue sedimentary rock, known locally as greywacke, which has been dated at 200 million years old. This range forms part of backbone chain that extends through most of the country.

In 1965 the Forest Amendment Act was passed and provided for setting aside sections of state forest as state forest parks to give them more protection. By 1971 eight areas, including Kaimanawa, were turned into state forest parks, administered by the NZFS that followed the multiple use concept.

GETTING STARTED

Tongariro is a national park with many access roads, good public transport and a wide range of tracks and huts. Visitors can enter the area from NH 1, SH 47, NH 4, or SH 49 as the four roads encase the outer boundaries. Most people travel to the Chateau to enjoy the park and first stop at the headquarters where information, maps and pamphlets are available along with an interesting display on the natural history of the area. From the Chateau there are a number of day walks to such popular spots as Taranaki Falls, Silica Rapids or the Tama Lakes. After two days on the track the park centre can also be a sudden jolt or a refreshing break for trampers passing through.

The complete Round-The-Mountain Track, possible from any of the four main access roads, is a long one with eight days or more of hard tramping through and over many gullies and ridges. A common tramp for most first-time hikers is from Ohakune Mountain Rd to SH 47, a five-day trip which highlights on the final day the best thermal area and the Ketetahi Hot Springs, excellent for relaxing any tight muscles. The walk for the most part stays above the bushline and offers incredible views, somewhat compensating for the occasional steep footwork. Although the track is rated medium, there is a great deal of climbing. Most of it is along well cut trails or well marked routes and can be attempted by trampers who are prepared to take their time.

Ohakune, a town of 1400 south of the park, is a jumping off spot for the five-day journey and can easily be reached from any direction by bus or rail. The town has supplies, a youth hostel to bed down in the night before, and information at a park ranger's station located at the foot of the Ohakune Mountain Rd (tel 578). The trailhead is close to the end of the mountain road, a drive of 20 km that ends at the 1585-metre level.

There is no bus service up the road. Those without private transport can either hire a costly taxi for the drive or hitch it. Hitchhiking, however, is uncertain. If successful it may leave you with a whole day in which to make the 1½-hour trip to the first hut; if unsuccessful the short trip to the hut from the trailhead is a blessing.

Transport at the other end is a little easier as you can hike from Ketetahi Hut to SH 47 in a couple of hours and then hitch to either Tokaanu or Turangi or maybe flag down the Hawkes Bay Motor bus as it passes through. The bus leaves in the early afternoon, stops at Turangi, passes the Ketetahi trailhead and then arrives at Chateau Tongariro in the late afternoon. In the opposite direction, the bus leaves National Park, a cross-roads town 15 km west of Chateau, each morning, stopping at the park headquarters and reaching Taupo late in the morning. There is no Sunday service. Tongariro is best walked during the period from November to mid-April. Because of the high altitude of the track, some wool clothing is needed no matter how warm and sunny the weather is when starting out.

The Kaimanawa trip described is a five-day tramp with hikes in alpine scrub on two of them. Trips in this forest are rated strenuous and trails should be attempted only by hikers with some back country experience. Although the tracks along this semi-circular trip have been recently cut and marked by the NZFS, trampers still have to be extra alert to avoid getting confused in many of the gullies and thick sections of beech bush. Before any trip you should stop in the NZFS office in Turangi (tel 7723) and outline your trip to the ranger in charge.

Public access to Kaimanawa has always been a problem. One legal and formed road gives access from the Napier-Taupo highway. Taharua Rd joins SH 5 some eight km north-west of Rangitaiki. Along this road about eight km and after a bridge over the Taharua river is the junction with Clements Rd (also known as Mill Rd). The trailhead to the first hut, Te Iringa, is six km along Clements Rd; the track rejoins the road a further 12 km along it.

Since most of Kaimanawa users are hunters, there is a preferred time to tramp there. From April to June is rutting season for deer, and large numbers of hunters come to the area, and to the huts at night. The ideal time for trampers is in mid-summer when the weather is at its best and the hunting is slow. However you might also want to pack along a tent as huts are limited in number and size.

Maps of both areas are published by the Department of Lands and Survey and are available through any office of the Government Printer. These are topographical maps of the NZMS 1 series. N111, N112, N121 and N122 cover Tongariro National Park; N103 and N113 cover the relevant section of Kaimanawa Forest Park. A recreational map of Tongariro National Park is also available.

TONGARIRO ROUND-THE-MOUNTAIN TRACK

The following trip is a walk that begins at Ohakune Mountain Rd and ends at SH 47, 64 km away. For those who want to turn the journey into a circular trip, it would be possible to return to Ohakune Mountain Rd by hiking on the eastern side of the volcanoes, through Rangipo Desert. The entire trip would be an eight to 10 day outing. If tramping from SH 47 south, allow more time for the hike up to Ketetahi Hut from the highway and less time for the walk from the hut to Mangatepopo Hut, which is 300 metres lower.

Ohakune Mountain Rd to Mangaturuturu Hut

At one point the mountain road passes through giant red beech trees and further up another winds through stunted forest. But at 1200 metres it leaves all bush behind and climbs into the alpine regions that Tongariro National Park is famous for. The road passes the park shelter hut after the bushline and then swings to the west at 1500 metres where a signpost points to the beginning of the track.

In a pattern that will become all too familiar by the end of the trip the track immediately drops into a gully and then climbs up a spur of bare rock and low-lying vegetation, marked by white poles that are weathered but still reassuring in a misty morning shower. From here, it descends steeply to the narrow bed of the south fork of the Mangaturuturu River, fording the mountain stream at one point across slippery lava rock where trampers should be extra sure-footed.

The slippery stream bed continues for a distance after the crossing before

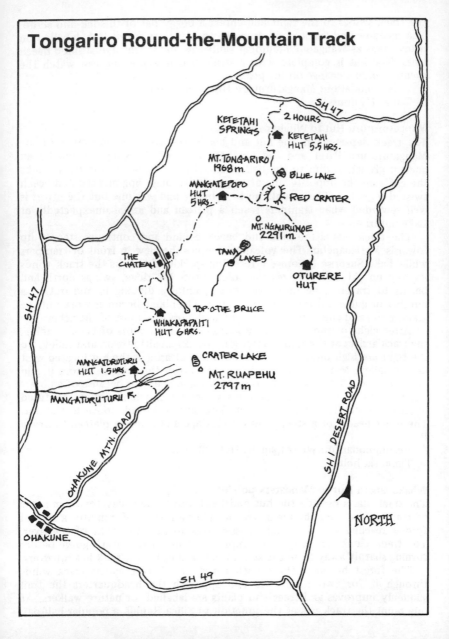

Tongariro Round-the-Mountain Track

SH 47

2 HOURS

KETETAHI SPRINGS

KETETAHI HUT 5.5 HRS.

MT. TONGARIRO 1968 m.

BLUE LAKE

MANGATEPOPO HUT 5 HRS.

RED CRATER

MT. NGAURUHOE 2291 m.

TAMA LAKES

THE CHATEAU

OTURERE HUT

TOP O THE BRUCE

WHAKAPAPAITI HUT 6 HRS.

SH 47

CRATER LAKE

MANGATURUTURU HUT 1.5 HRS.

MT. RUAPEHU 2797 m

MANGATURUTURU R.

SH 1 DESERT ROAD

OHAKUNE MTN. ROAD

NORTH

OHAKUNE.

SH 49

the track swings to the right and enters a boggy flat of tussock and scrub. The meadow and track slope down to the Mangaturuturu Hut, labelled on many maps as Wanganui Tramping Club Hut, in the fringe of stunted beech trees. The hut is complete with a stone bench where one can watch the evening colours change on the peak.

Accommodation: Mangaturuturu Hut, eight bunks
Time: 1½ hours

Mangaturuturu Hut to Whakapapaiti Hut

The track departs from the hut and heads west to the main branch of the Mangaturuturu River and the northern edge of the gully created by an ancient glacier. It dips to the bed of the stream, crosses it and then climbs the cliffs on the opposite side after passing through bog and stunted beech twisted togetlher. The ascent can be a bushy and wet one but the effort is well rewarded when trampers reach a plateau and arrive unexpectedly at Lake Surprise.

The track leaves the lake and beech behind and continues steeply up towards Mt Ruapehu. The volcano occupies the view in front of trampers while Lake Surprise becomes a receding sparkle of blue as the track winds its way up. At 1500 metres the track meets the ridge, swings north and begins to traverse the mountain side, painfully dipping in and out of a number of gullies all the way to the hut. The hiking becomes work but the grand views and enjoyable alpine scrub and moss ease most of the aches.

After eight or more stream crossings and three hours of back bending, the track arrives at the spur overlooking Whakapapaiti Stream and valley. To the right are high mountain bluffs but more pleasing is the hut located west in the valley. Marker poles lead the way down the stream, across it and eventually to a signposted junction. After a long day or because of an over-eagerness to get to the hut, trampers sometimes momentarily get confused in this section. At the junction the left-hand fork leads south to the hut. The other heads for a steep climb up a ridge and across a plateau to Bruce Rd.

Accommodation: Whakapapaiti Hut, 22 bunks
Time: six hours

Whakapapaiti Hut to Mangatepopo Hut

The track starts outside the hut and heads down the valley for 30 minutes to reach a ford over the main stream. After a further 30 minutes a second ford is reached and the track crosses back to the true right of the river. The track climbs shortly to an impressive view of the river's gorge before turning sharply away from the stream and heading for the park headquarters.

The forest becomes thick with a variety of trees as the track winds through it for two hours. As you approach the headquarters the trail suddenly improves and trees and plants are labelled for nature walkers. At one point the track passes the junction to Silica Rapids, a popular half-day hike from the headquarters, then crosses a bridge to eventually arrive at the motor camp on the edge of the service centre.

An alternative route from Whakapapaiti Hut is to head back to the junction encountered the previous day and follow the steep zig-zag track to the ridge and the Bruce Rd. From here it is a short walk (or hitch) to Top-O-The-Bruce where many hikers follow the ski runs and chair lifts to the top of Mt Ruapehu. The climb makes for a long day for the most experienced trampers so it is best to stay at the Chateau for the night. Accommodation available includes hotel, motel and motor camp styles; at times a special rate for youth hostellers is available from the motel.

From the Chateau, the terrain changes dramatically from the thick bush to rolling tussock grasslands that are a pleasure to hike through after fighting gullies the day before. At first the track is well marked and beched for day hikers but gradually reverts to marker poles as it cuts across the tussock. Mt Ngauruhoe dominates the view to the right, the cone of Pukeonake is on the left, and behind you are the chimneys and drifting smoke of the Chateau Hotel. Finally the track gently ascends a spur from which trampers can spot the access road below and at its end, Mangatepopo Hut.

Accommodation: Mangatepopo Hut, 24 bunks

Time: five hours

Mangatepopo Hut to Ketetahi Hut

From the hut there is a sighposted track that leads off to the 1954 lava flows and makes an interesting side trip. The main track sidles along between lava flows and the Mangatepopo Stream until it reaches a steep climb to the saddle between Mt Ngauruhoe and Mt Tongariro. The climb is marked by poles and swings back and forth until finally reaching a saddle, 1653 metres above sea level. At this point hikers with extra energy can drop their packs and scramble to the summit of Mt Ngauruhoe, a 2½-hour climb up and about a 30-minute slide down. Beware of loose scoria and falling rocks dislodged by other climbs.

The track leaves the saddle and moves into the most interesting section of the track. It first cuts through the lunar-like South Crater and then from the far side, climbs along a poled route to the edge of Red Crater, the highest point of the track at 1820 metres. Here the steam and unique colour of the crater or the brilliance of Emerald Lakes is an excuse for most trampers to take an extended break. Others might take the side trail to the summit of Mt Tongariro, an hour trip that will lead to excellent views of the thermal activity.

The track continues down sliding cinders along the edge of Red Crater and heads towards Central Crater, passing the lakes along the way. It levels out at Central Crater and crosses it to reach Blue Lake on the other side. After skirting around the lake, the track passes over a saddle and then follow a series of switchbacks. It leaves the bare rock of the craters and descends steeply into tussock and eventually arrives at the Ketetahi Hut.

The view from the hut is immense as one can look to the north and see Lake Rotoaira, Mt Pihanga or Lake Taupo. The sunsets are beautiful and the hot springs, a short distance away, relaxing. This is definitely one place where an extra day should be spent.

Accommodation: Ketetahi Hut, 24 bunks

Time: 5½ hours

Ketetahi Hut to SH 47

The last section of the trip begins in tussock at first, passing the steaming springs and then descends sharply into a forest of totara and cabbage trees. Once in the bush, it levels out, crosses and recrosses a small branch of the Mangatipua Stream and emerges out of the shady Okahukura bush at the car park on the access road off SH 47.

For those who want to continue around the eastern side of the volcanoes, backtrack over the saddle to Blue Lake and take the south-eastern fork at the sighnposted junction before Emerald Lakes. This track heads for Oturere Hut, a five to six hour walk from Ketetahi Hut.

Time: two hours

KAIMANAWA STATE FOREST

The following trip description begins at the trailhead to Te Iringa Hut from Clements Rd just past Te Arero Stream. It ends when the track from Cascade Hut reaches the end of Clements Rd. Those without transport can continue on Clements Rd for a further four km on the final day and spend the night at one of the camping sites. The following day would be spent hiking along to Taharua Rd and then to SH 5.

Clements Rd to Te Iringa Hut

The trailhead is located off Clements Rd after it crosses Te Arero Stream. The track is signposted, well marked and benched all of the way to the hut. It is easily graded for about 15 minutes' hiking, then climbs for about 45 minutes through thick bush, gradually becoming steeper. Te Iringa Hut is on the right. It is small, with only six bunks, but has an open fireplace and is a welcome sight for trampers who have had to hike to the trailhead. Te Iringa Hut is small, holds only six bunks and has an open fireplace. But it is a welcome site for trampers who had to hike a portion of the vehicle track to the trailhead.

Accommodation: Te Iringa Hut, six bunks

Time: 1½ hours

Te Iringa Hut to Oamaru Hut

The track leaves the hut and continues on the ridge, climbing to pass north of the summit. It swings to the east, dips over another spur and then gradually descends to ford the Tiki Tiki Stream.

The track follows the true left bank of the stream until the junction of

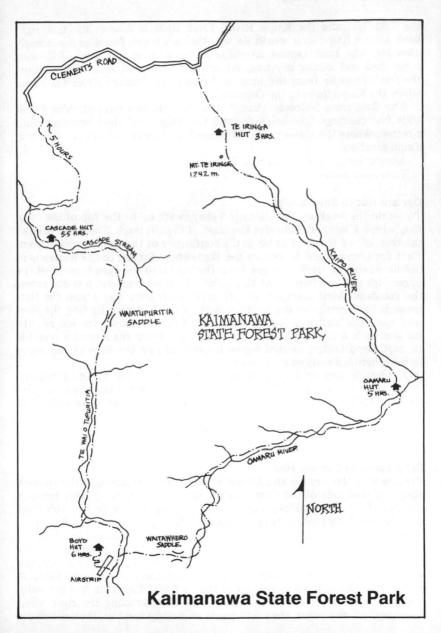

Kaimanawa State Forest Park

the Tiki Tiki and the Kaipo River. From there it follows the true right bank of the Kaipo as it works its way through beech forest in a southerly direction. The track crosses several small branches of the Kaipo, following a benched and usually dry trail. After a two-hour walk from the junction, the track emerges from the bush and enters the Oamaru River Flats near where the Kaipo flows in the Oamaru.

The flats are a welcome change in flora after two days of thick forest with few clearings. The track follows the Kaipo and then branches onto a terrace where the Oamaru Hut is located, 200 metres above the Oamaru-Kaipo junction.

Accommodation: Oamaru Hut, 16 bunks
Time: five hours

Oamaru Hut to Boyd Lodge

To locate the track up the Oamaru Valley, walk up to the top of the open flats where a signpost indicates the start of the cut track. The track follows the true left of the river as far as the confluence of the Waitawhero Stream. Ford the Oamaru and follow up the Waitawhero Stream to the Waitawhero Saddle where the track emerges from the bush into the open tussock of the upper Ngaruro catchment. At this point, the track becomes a route across the grassland. Most trampers simply make their own way across the flats towards the airstrip on the western bank of the Ngaruro, fording the river with care. The airstrip is less than one hour from the saddle; the hut next to the airstrip is a privately-owned hunting lodge. From the strip it is possible to spot Boyd Lodge, located below Boyd Rocks on the edge of the beech forest. There is a marked route on it.

A possible side trip from Boyd Hut is to scale Mt Tapuiomaruahine (1331 metres), an easy climb from the hut and one that provides good views of Mt Makorako to the west and the peaks of Tongariro National Park beyond.

Accommodation: Boyd Lodge, 16 bunks
Time: six hours

Boyd Lodge to Cascade Hut

Backtrack to the airstrip and follow an old horse trail through the tussock along the west side of the Ngaruro River as the track makes its way through the river flats and gradually curves west. Trampers have to be extra alert on this stretch to avoid getting confused or losing their sense of direction. Search for the route markings and check a map regularly during the day.

Eventually the Ngaruro arrives at a junction with five or six smaller streams leading off in several directions. One is the Te Wai O Tupuritia, the only stream departing due north, which can be reached after several fords. A route exists through the river flats of the Te Wai O Tupuritia, but generally trampers make their own way through the area, crossing the river when necessary. At one point, the route passes an airstrip and hut, then continues until it reaches the forest edge again. Here a marked and cut track gradually ascends to the Waiatupuritia Saddle, crosses it then descends to a branch of the Cascade Stream. The track descends quickly along the small stream to its junction with the main branch of the Cascade.

In the last leg of the tramp, the track begins to swing to a westerly direction, following the Cascade Stream and finally ascends to the hut near the junction with the Taupo River.

Accommodation: Cascade Hut, six bunks

Time: 5½ hours

Cascade Hut to Clements Rd

To return to the end of Clements Rd, depart from the hut and travel down the Taurango-Taupo River for 20 minutes on the true right bank.

Here a cut track begins working up a valley in a gradual ascent. Eventually it leads over a saddle and then descends the rest of the way to the end of Clements Rd, following another stream most of the way. In this section, the track becomes an old hunter's trail; take care so as not to get confused along the way.

From the end of the road, it is another four km to the Waiharuru Hut, where trampers can spend the night before heading out the next morning.

Time: five hours

North Island — south

Tararua State Forest Park

North of Wellington there is a place where the wind dances on the mountainsides and the fog creeps silently in the early morning. It is where gales might hurl their weight through steep river gorges, snow might fall lightly on sharp greywacke peaks or rain could trickle down both sides of a ridge that is tightrope narrow.

It is also where stormy Wellington likes to play.

Tararua State Forest Park and Wellington go hand in hand. For years it was almost an exclusive weekend retreat for hikers and hunters from the windly city and surrounding area. Today trampers from around the country are attracted to the park's broken terrain and the sheerness of its features that present a challenge to the most experienced backpackers. But being only 50 km north of Wellington, the Tararuas will always remain the quick escape for those who live in the city but belong in the woods.

The park is centred on the Tararua Range that stretches for 80 km north of Wellington to the Manawatu Gorge, a natural gap that separates it from the Ruahine Range. The tallest peak is Mitre, 1571 metres, and many more are close to that height. In between there are ridges and spurs that are renowned for being narrow, steep and razor sharp.

The land is rugged but the wind, fog and rain have become the park's trademark's. They are notorious. The entire park is exposed to westerly winds that funnel through the gap between New Zealand's two great islands. The range is the first thing the air streams hit and they hit it in full force, smacking against the high ridges and peaks. At times it is almost impossible for a person to stand up in the winds, especially with a 15 or 20 kg pack.

A   Mt Ruapehu, the highest mountain in the North Island, in Tongariro National Park

B   The start of the New Zealand Walkway from Cape Reinga in the North Island to Bluff in the South Island

The predominant wind is from the west or north-west and usually is blowing during the summer. Calms or gentle breezes are rare.

So are clear mountain tops. On the average the summits and peaks are fog-bound two days out of three or are clear less than 100 days of the year. The western side of the park can be even worse as it records the most clouds and fog and the least amount of sunshine. Rain averages around 1500 mm in the lowlands, 2500 mm in the foothills and often exceeds 5000 mm above the bushline. Snow may lie above 1200 metres three to four months of the year and a snow storm can be expected any time on the alpine ridges and peaks.

But it is the sudden storms, fierce and full of rain, that set Tararua apart from other parks in the country. They arrive with very little for warning and have dumped as much as 333 mm of rain on a single day. Perhaps the most devastating one was in 1936 when the wind was so severe that trees were reported snapped off or yanked off by their roots and carried through the air.

There is a good variety of flora in the state park where many plants reach their southern limits. The forest is predominantly beech with scattered rimu and northern rata found in the lower altitudes and mostly silver beech as the timberline species. There is a dense understorey of ferns, mosses and supplejack in the wet western sections where the park is heavily forested with few clearings below 900 metres.

Above 1200 metres, the forest gives way to open alpine vegetation of snow tussock, snowgrass and scree. Much of the alpine grasslands have been severely affected by introduced animals. Deer depend heavily on the alpine regions for food and have depleted the tussock in height and cover. Together with goats and opossums they have severely affected the undergrowth in the forested regions and accelerated erosion.

The native birdlife is present and widespread but well concealed in the bush, making it appear limited in variety and numbers. Bellbirds, tuis and New Zealand pigeons are common and easy to spot while the rifleman, pied fantail, whitehead and grey warbler require a more observant eye. There is also the bush hawk, which is well distributed throughout the park and has taken its toll of smaller birds. Near the rivers, you can

A Torrent Bay along the Abel Tasman Coastal Track
B A swing bridge on the Abel Tasman Coastal Track

occasionally spot grey ducks, black shags and black-backed gulls.

The state forest park has a long history with trampers, resulting today in a vast network of tracks and routes throughout the area and over 60 huts and shelters for overnight use. Being at Wellington's backdoor, the Tararuas have become the local stamping ground for hikers from the capital city in much the same way Abel Tasman is to trampers from Nelson. Because of the capricious weather and the broken terrain, trampers have to be prepared and experienced to undertake any long treks into the heart of the park. The tracks for the most part are well marked, with footbridges over the more difficult rivers. Many routes follow open ridges and are steep sided and narrow, so trampers have to be careful. Where the ridge forks or confusion is possible, the NZFS has placed stakes or cairns to aid hikers.

Mainly trips into the park involve a good deal of climbing, but several day hikes are possible that give access to the Tararua Range to inexperienced trampers or those who don't want to grunt for three or four days up a ridge. A good place for day hiking is the Mt Holdsworth Lodge area, off of SH 2 and 18 km from Masterton. From the Lodge, there are possible day hikes to Donnelly Flat, Rocky Lookout, Mountain House or for the energetic, Mt Holdsworth itself, a 4½-hour climb to the top.

The park also offers what are commonly known as 'gorge trips' for adventurers who need more than a breath-taking climb along a ridge. Gorge trips involve riding an air mattress or an inner tube from a car tyre down several rivers that have carved steep gorges in the Tararua Range. This involves actually swimming or wading while still wearing boots and hauling a pack along. Plastic bags are used to keep all gear dry but most gorge trips are followed by a drying out session at the end. Among the rivers that trampers can swim are sections of the Otaki, Waiotauru, Hector, Mangahao, Waiohine and Ohau.

HISTORY

The foundations of the Tararua range were laid down in a deep sea basin some 200 million years ago. Earth movements along a series of faults, one of which is an extension of the fault that runs through Wellington and the Hutt valley, resulted in a complicated mass of folded and faulted rock. Uplift of the land and subsequent erosion by the elements, including an ice age, have resulted in the rugged range that separates the rolling Wairarapa district from the west coast.

Today the Tararua Range separates the farm pastures of Wairarapa from the west coast. It's too remote and rugged for any settlement but in pre-European days the Maoris did use a couple of routes to pass through it to the west coast. One crosses the Mangahao River and another was believed to be over Arawara, a low peak in the northern section of the range.

European explorers began to penetrate the dense bush in 1844 but it was not until 1863 that J C Crawford climbed Mt Dennan with a Maori guide for the first recorded venture in the alpine regions of the range.

With the discovery of gold throughout the country in the 1860s, prospectors also eyed the Tararuas as an area to strike it rich. The precious metal lured in many prospecting parties during the era which struggled over the ridges and panned the streams. Small quantities were reported from 1862 to 1887 but never in amounts worth mining for.

Government surveyors were the next group of explorers. They began charting the area in the late 1860s and by 1881 had produced a map of the range. Though the entire area had not been explored, track clubs began forming in 1880 to provide access to the wilderness back-country. One of the earliest was the Greytown-Mt Hector Tourist Track Committee, which was active in cutting tracks and constructing huts. The construction of more tracks, huts and one suspension bridge took place over the next 30 years. In 1919 the Tararua Tramping Club was formed to promote expeditions into the range.

The importance of the Tararuas as the watershed for Wellington's future water supply was recognised early in its history. In the late 1880s, much concern over forest fires was directed to the Department of Lands and Survey while Coleman Phillips, a Wairarapa station owner, urged the government in 1896 to reserve the area as a watershed. Today the scars of past fires are barely visible except for the 1938 burn on Marchant Ridge. This blaze left a mass of black stumps that can still be seen about Dobson Hut.

Protection for the park began in 1919 when the State Forest Service was established and a move began to reserve a section of the Tararuas that was originally purchased from the Maoris in 1871. In 1936, there was a proposal to turn the area into a national park as a memorial for the Wellington Province centennial but it lost out to setting aside Petone Beach. Popularity of the area, especially among the trampers, picked up after World War II and in 1952 another proposal to turn Tararua into a national park was submitted. This time the government chose its new system of land management and reserved the area as New Zealand's first state forest park.

Today the NZFS maintains the tracks and its own system of huts, free for anybody to use. But its primary interest is not recreation, rather the protection of Wellington's watershed as the agency attempts this by reducing soil erosion and regulating water run-off.

GETTING STARTED

Although Tararua State Forest Park is the playground for Wellington, there are a number of places to outfit an expedition and gain access into the mountain range. The most popular departing point is Mt Holdsworth, a highly developed area with a lodge, picnic grounds, car park, and permanent caretaker who can assist with the right information. The facilities are located at the end of Norfolk Rd off SH 2 at Waingawa on the eastern edge of the park. From the western side, the best access is from either Manakau via the North Manakau Rd or the Akatarawa Hill Rd which leads to a 20-km long logging track into the park.

For the trip described the access point is Kaitoke, a small town 16 km north of Upper Hutt on SH 2. After crossing the Pakurahi Bridge, turn left on Marchant Rd and follow it for three km to the park entrance sign and the Kaitoke Shelter and car park beyond. Here one of the park's better known trails, the Puffer Track, begins.

Because of the limited size of Kaitoke, the best place to outfit the trip is Upper Hutt, where not only supplies are available but also information and transportation. The information is at the NZFS Office where you can ask questions, receive answers and purchase such handy publications as the *Tararua Forest Park Hunting and Recreation Guide* or the *Tararua Forest Park Route Guide*. Other NZFS offices that can supply information on the area are in Wellington, Palmerston North, Masterton and Manakau. The permanent caretaker of Mt Holdsworth lives in a house close to the lodge.

Transport to Mt Kaitoke is available from either direction asn the NZ Railways Road Service has a daily bus from Wellington to Masterton that will drop you off at the Kaitoke Post Office and Youth Hostel. The bus run connects with several inter-island ferry arrivals from Picton in which case it is usually easiest to spend the night at the youth hostel for a fresh start. Here additional information about the tracks and possibly even tramping partners or transportation to the trailhead can be obtained.

It is possible to take the train to Upper Hutt and then hitch to Kaitoke as traffic is frequent along SH 2 during the summer and fair the rest of the year.

If you have your own vehicle, there is a convenient car park at the start of the track. It is also at the end of the circular route, eliminating the hassle of having to find a way back to the car that other tracks involve.

The described trek is rated strenuous as are most overnight tramps deep into the state forest park. Trampers have to be prepared for the adventure with the right equipment and physical stamina. Sudden changes of weather can turn a sunny, pleasant day into one of rain, gusty winds or even snow with little forewarning. Necessary equipment includes warm clothing, mittens and a hat to prevent loss of body heat due to exposure when caught in foul conditions. A map and compass should also be carried and at least one member of the party should have a working knowledge of them as fog and clouds will often cut down visibility considerably. This is not a trek for tennis shoes or flimsy boots. Good hiking boots, that are well broken in, are needed for the rugged terrain. Above all, rain gear, both parka and pants, should be at the top of every tramper's pack.

If your group is considering taking a gorge trip, every member will need either an inflatable rubber mattress or a tyre inner tube. You will also need a good supply of plastic bags. Zip-lock bags work best although they are extremely hard to find in New Zealand supermarkets. Everything in a backpack should be in a plastic bag which should be twisted and knotted at the opening. This not only helps to keep equipment dry but also adds bouyancy. No matter how carefully you wrap everything and tie your pack, every gorge trip needs a full drying-out session. Accept it, it's inevitable.

Just about everyone has their own special technique when travelling the rivers and part of the fun is to master your own, but swimmers should keep their boots on to avoid bruises from the rough river bottom, and most do not wear their packs as they tend to float up the back and push the head down.

One last item you should pack is extra days — with rations. If adverse weather pops up, it is better to wait it out in the comfort of a hut instead of pushing on because of a time limitation.

The 'Tararua State Forest Park Hunting and Recreation Guide' is an adequate map of the area with a scale of 1:100,000. Many trampers, however, prefer the series one topographical maps N157 and N152 which cover the entire state forest park.

TRACK DESCRIPTION

The following trek is a six-day trip that includes ridge walking and a one-day gorge trip from Mid Waiohine Hut to Totara Flats Hut along the Waiohine River. To skip the swim or to take in more alpine hiking, it is possible to tramp up Mt Holdsworth and then follow the Totara Creek to Totara Flats in one day.

Kaitoke Shelter to Alpha Hut

An early start is a must! This section includes a few steep climbs and being the first day, most trampers have to take plenty of rest stops. From the Kaitoke Shelter, a four-wheel-drive vehicle track ascends up the neighbouring spur for 30 minutes before reaching a signposted junction. The right-hand fork is to Puffer Saddle, about 800 metres away, while the left-hand one is the Marchant Ridge Track which continues up the spur to the ridge top.

There is good hiking on the top of the ridge as it levels out along a section covered with low scrub before climbing sharply again through bush to Dobson Hut. Before the hut, however, the track passes rows of burnt tree stumps, the remaining evidence of a severe forest fire in 1938. The hut, two hours from the start, is a good place for a mid-morning break before tackling the next climb.

The track works its way on the side of Marchant Ridge while always climbing steadily through fire-scarred areas. After an hour the track begins its final ascent of Mt Marchant and reaches the 1038-metre summit before dipping into bush again. The trail continues on the ridge, past Axehole (a dried-up waterhole) and then arrives at the junction with Block XVI Track, a steep descent to the Tauherenikau River.

The track continues on the ridge with a sharp drop followed by a mild climb to the beginning of the Golden Stairs. This steep ascent ends at Mt Omega (1118 metres) where the track swings west along a flat boggy open section of the ridge. A steep drop takes trampers over a saddle

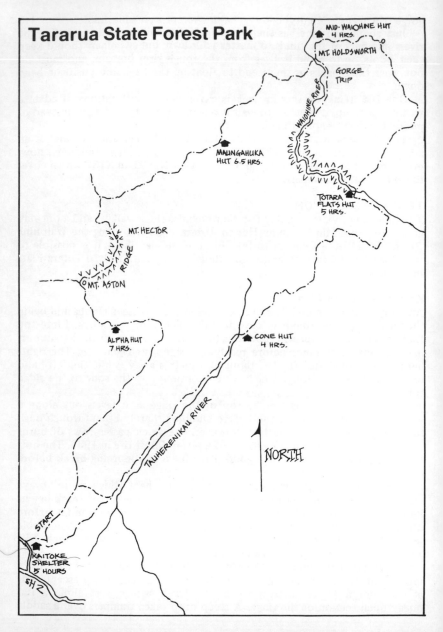

Tararua State Forest Park

MID-WAIOHINE HUT
4 HRS.

MT. HOLDSWORTH

GORGE
TRIP

WAIOHINE RIVER

MAUNGAHUKA
HUT 6.5 HRS.

TOTARA
FLATS HUT
5 HRS.

MT. HECTOR

RIDGE

MT. ASTON

ALPHA HUT
7 HRS.

CONE HUT
4 HRS.

TAUHERENIKAU RIVER

NORTH

START

KAITOKE
SHELTER
5 HOURS

SH 2

and a slight climb leads them past Hells Gate. A little more up and down climbing and the track swings north of the ridge to Alpha Hut.

Accommodation: Alpha Hut, 20 bunks

Time: seven hours

Alpha Hut to Maungahuka Hut

The track departs from the hut and climbs through a bush of leatherworks to the summit of Mt Alpha and its open alpine fields. The descent of the peak is along a spur to the north-west that leads down to a saddle where the track begins working its way up Mt Aston (1378 metres). The summit is reached on the eastern side around a slip.

At Aston there is a junction with the left-hand fork leading west to Elder Bivouac. To the right, the route continues along Marchant Ridge. Here the ridge opens up and resumes climbing. After crossing a hump and passing a tarn, the track begins its climb to Mt Atkinson, a lengthy tramp to its 1461-metre summit. Following Mt Atkinson, there are two steep climbs, the first one to the Beehives and the second to Mt Hector, 2½ hours from Alpha Hut.

Mt Hector at 1529 metres is the highest peak in the southern portion of the park and in good weather offers a spectacular view of the surrounding countryside. It is also a junction with one route departing north-east for Winchcombe Bivouac and the other along a north-west ridge to descend to a saddle and then climb to Field Peak. The north-west ridge continues down past Kime Hut, over Hut Mound at 1431 metres and down again to New Kime Hut below Bridge Peak.

The ridge that leads off to the north-east is known by most local trampers as the Main Range and includes a route from Bridge Peak to Mt Crawford. This section of it includes several tarns and humps and then climbs over Boyd Wilson Knowll and the peaks of Mt Vosseler, Mt Yeates and Mt McIntosh. If that wasn't enough for a person, one of the steepest climbs of the day follows when the ridge route ascends to the first of the two Tararua Peaks and the tallest at 1330 metres.

From the top, trampers should descend along the west side to a rib, cross it after seven metres and descend further to a rock wall and the chain ladder at the end. From here it is possible to climb down to the bottom before having to tramp around the second peak to a sharp ridge that leads to Mt Maungahuka (1329 metres). The Maungahuka Hut is reached after crossing the peak and walking to the south end of the tarn.

Accommodation: Maungahuka Hut, six bunks

Time: 6½ hours

Maungahuka Hut to Mid Waiohine Hut

The route continues along the Main Range with easy descents and climbs over Mt Simpson and Mt Wright as it loses altitude along the way. Scrub reappears when the long trek to the top of Mt Aokaparangi begins. The trek to the 1346-metre summit ends at the junction with the track to the Waiohine River, two hours from the Maungahuka Hut.

The track leads quickly down and away from the Alpine areas of Mt Aokaparangi into the bush again. The track levels out somewhat from the beginning but continues to descend until it reaches the Waiohine River. Here it crosses a footbridge and turns sharply north to travel upstream a short distance to Mid Waiohine Hut. The NZFS hut is on the east side of the river and sleeps six.

Accommodation: Mid Waiohine Hut, six bunks
Time: four hours

Mid Waiohine Hut to Totara Flats via Waiohine Gorge

Trampers not equipped with a rubber mattress or tyre inner tube can avoid the gorge trip by hiking east to Mt Isabelle and then on to Mt Holdsworth (1470 metres), a three hour tramp uphill. From there they can turn south and follow the Mt Holdsworth Track to Powell Hut, cross Pig Flat and then cut south-west to descend gradually along Totara Creek to its junction with the Waiohine River. The alternative route would take between four and five hours and offer scenic views from the top of Mt Holdsworth.

For those who choose to swim the river, backtrack south to the footbridge and then beyond for two more hours when the 'bad gorge' begins. The steep gorge is marked by two large slips on both sides. There is a small pool before it where most trampers put in their floatation device. Travelling down a gorge consists of swimming through the deeper pools and sections of the river and wading in the shallow ones. From here the terrain turns into one of the most spectacular gorges in the park as the sides close in and at one point the trees 30 metres overhead almost connect one side to the other. The river doesn't enter the open valley until it curves east and reaches Hector Forks, an hour after putting in the water.

Travel continues in the river with a handful of pools to swim but the going is easy and in an hour from Hector Forks the current sweeps past Totara Flats. At the hut here you can dry out all equipment and clothing for the tramp the following day.

Accommodation: Totara Flats Hut, 20 bunks
Time: five hours

Totara Flats to Cone Hut

The track resumes south from Totara Flats, skirting the bush and eventually moving into the wide open area of the flats where trampers pretty much have to pick and choose their own way through this section. It is best to stay close to the river's edge, however, to avoid the swamps below the hill. At one point the NZFS hut, Totara Lodge, pops up and a little further on another one, Sayers Hut, appears across the river next to Sayers Stream. Just before the high bluff at the southern end of the flat, the track swings to the west and climbs up a steep bank to a terrace.

The track works around the bluff and then back to the river where it crosses a rocky section beneath the cliff and continues downstream to Makaka Creek, marked by a distinct S-shaped bend in the Waiohine. Just past the creek the track swings west and follows the stream a short distance before splitting off to a spur that drops into a saddle. From the first saddle, the track climbs to a second one, Cone Saddle at 546 metres, after swinging to a more southerly direction. Some trampers make the mistake of heading straight and end up scaling Mt Cone.

From Cone Saddle, the track drops steeply to Cone Hut, on the east side of the Tauherenikau River, a 20-minute descent. The hut is across from a large slip which has a good swimming hole at its down-stream corner.

Accommodation: Cone Hut, 12 bunks

Time: four hours

Cone Hut to Kaitoke Shelter

The track follows the eastern shore of the river beyond the hut. After an hour from Cone Hut, the track arrives at a junction with the Mt Reeves Track and then passes the Tutuwai Hut further south before arriving at a wirewalk that crosses the Tauherenikau to the west shore.

From here it is a scamble up the steep bank to a well-defined track that keeps to the west shore for another hour and a half until Smith Creek Shelter where the Tauherenikau curves sharply to the east. The main track follows Smith Creek and passes the shelter on the opposite shore. The track begins its ascent to Puffer Saddle and crosses Smith Creek a few times before sharply climbing the last section to the pass. At the saddle one track heads north to Marchant Ridge while the other one leads about west one km to a level ridge, then down to Kaitoke Shelter and along the first spur of the trip.

Time: five hours

South Island — north-west

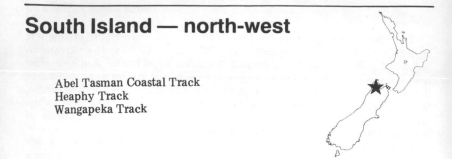

Abel Tasman Coastal Track
Heaphy Track
Wangapeka Track

It's a big jump from the North Island to the north-west corner of the South Island. More than most trampers expect.

Gone are the volcanoes and thermal activity of Tongariro and Egmont National Parks, not yet arrived are the world-renowned Southern Alps and the surrounding alpine regions. Far off in the distance are the misty sounds and spectacular waterfalls of Fiordland. What one stumbled upon in this isolated part of the country is all its own — incredibly thick bush, extraordinarily beautiful beaches, swaying palm trees and, surprisingly, areas that receive more sun than rain.

Part of the region has been preserved in two main parks, the North-West Nelson State Forest Park and the Abel Tasman National Park. Situated away from large population centres and main road access, the area was pushed into the limelight when plans for a road along the Heaphy Track sparked an intense controversy. Environmental concerns and opposition to the road proposal generated a wide interest in the track which runs south of Collingwood to the West Coast. Today it is one of the few tracks that can come close to the Milford in annual usage.

But the Heaphy is generally an exception. Most of the area experiences few periods of summer crowding. Some parts of the Abel Tasman have not yet even been explored, and one of its major waterfalls was discovered only in recent years. It is this isolation from roads, cities and the steady flow of tour buses that appeals to trampers who choose to undertake any of these tracks.

Then there is the terrain. It is New Zealand, but a step away from the rest of the country. North-West Nelson State Forest Park, of 358,841 hectares, is 83% forest and bush — thick, lush and subtropical in nature. There are mountain ranges in the park, with one peak rising over 1826 metres, but they are lost to the golden beaches and nikau palms that line the Tasman Sea. The same holds true for Abel Tasman. Most of the park is dense forest situated in rugged and hilly terrain; but it is the numerous bays, beaches and isolated inlets that attract the attention of visitors and hikers. And it is the sun that keeps them returning. The coastal region experiences only 125 days of rain a year, resulting in long dry spells from summer through fall that are so uncommon in much of the South Island.

There are dozens of tracks and track combinations in this region of New Zealand but three are longtime favourites with Kiwi trampers. The Heaphy, a four or five-day hike that includes a stretch along the golden sand of the Tasman Sea, ranges 76 km from Karamea to the junction of the Brown and Aorere rivers, not far from Collingwood. The nearby Wangapeka Track is a harder five-day trip from the Rolling River beyond Tapawera, up the Wangapeka River and along the Little Wanganui, finishing near the mouth of the river on the West Coast. The third, and my favourite, is one of the most beautiful coastal trails in the country but is hardly known outside the Nelson area. The Abel Tasman coastal track is a four or five-day trip that hugs the bays and beaches of the national park north from Marahau, skirts south of Separation Point and ends at the farm road that leads to Takaka in the Golden Bay district.

Both the Heaphy and the Wangapeka lie almost entirely in the North-West State Forest Park, an area with an eastern boundary 100 km west of Nelson. The state forest is noted for its rainforest bush but also contains alpine herbfields, rocky peaks and rolling stretches of red tussock; the most spectacular being the Gouland Downs. Beech forest covers most of the hills while rimu and other podocarps are found on the lower slopes in the western section of the park. They support a thick undergrowth of broad-leaf, kamahi and ferns.

The park is the home of five major river systems and many lakes, all fed by the westerly winds off the Tasman Sea that bring up to 5000 mm of rain per year to the mountainous areas. The rest of the park also experiences large doses of rain while frost is possible in the higher exposed regions, particularly the Gouland Downs, in spring, early summer or fall. The Wangapeka Saddle, where a rain gauge is maintained, recorded over 500 mm of rain in January, 1964. The yearly average for most of the track is around 2540 mm.

The Abel Tasman Coast Track lies almost entirely in the national park, a reserve of 22,370 hectares and New Zealand's smallest national park. The area is a temperate rainforest, characterized by thick bush in the western inland sections and beech forests around the coastal fringes. All five species of beech are found in this national park, and the country's national plant, the silver fern, is found in abundance all along the track.

Protection by mountain ranges from southerly and westerly winds gives the park the best weather in the country. Extreme temperatures are rare in the mild and sunny climate of Abel Tasman while rainfall averages 1250 mm along the coast and 2540 mm in the highlands. Frosts are rare on the coast, occurring only occasionally during early or late winter.

Both parks have strong bird populations that include good numbers of the weka and South Island kiwi, tui, bellbird, blue mountain duck, parakeet, kingfisher, black oystercatcher and even the southern blue penguin in areas of Abel Tasman. Reports of sightings of the rare kakapo have been made in North-West Nelson State Forest Park but never confirmed. The beaches and inlets of both regions thrive with shellfish: mussels, pipis and paua, that provide a delicious dinner for the adventurous.

One of the most unusual animals found in both parks is the rare carni-vorous snail. It has been known to grow to lengths of eight cm and is easily identified by its rich mahogany-coloured shell. Collecting these snails or their shells is prohibited. You may also find large creamy bush worms along the Gouland Downs or, if extremely lucky, spot long or short-eared bats, the only mammals native to New Zealand. Both areas also contain the introduced animals such as red deer, opossums, a few goats and wild pigs.

There is good fishing for the angler with brown trout in all major rivers of the North-West Nelson State Forest Park, particularly the Karamea and Wangapeka Rivers, and rainbow trout in Cobb River and the Cobb hydro reservoir. Along the beach stretch of the Heaphy track there is excellent shore fishing.

HISTORY

The legendary moa thrived in the north-west region of the South Island and this important food source led to the establishment of a significant Maori population by the 13th century.

Abel Tasman anchored his ships off Separation Point in 1642, but in an incident with the local Maoris four sailors were killed. Cook stopped briefly in 1770 but recorded little information of the coastal area and nothing of its inhabitants. It wasn't until Dumont D'Urville sailed into the area in 1827 that Europeans engaged these Maoris on peaceful terms. The French navig-ator made friends with the villagers as he studied flora and wildlife and charted the bays and inlets of the northern coast. But while European involvement in the area grew, tribal wars and introduced diseases led to a serious reduction in the Maori popultion. Within 50 years, five centuries of Maori heritage and tradition were almost erased from history.

Exploration continued in 1846 when 23-year-old Charles Heaphy and Thomas Brunner became the first Europeans to hike up the west coast to the Heaphy River. During the four-month expedition on the coast the pair were told by their Maori guides of open tussock grasslands (Gouland Downs) and the Maori route across the interior to Golden Bay. Neither Heaphy nor Brunner made it up the Heaphy River, however, to search for the passage. James MacKay and John Clark followed to complete the inland portion of the Heaphy Track in 1860 on a search for gold betwen Buller and Colling-wood. A year later gold was discovered at Karamea, inspiring prospectors to struggle over the track to search for it.

Settlement began in the early 1850s in the area that was to become the Abel Tasman National Park. The new settlers ranged from farmers and fish-ermen to shipwrights and timber millers but by far the most enterprising one was William Gibbs. The estate and mansion he built at Totaranui and the innovations he implemented there were way ahead of his time. Gibbs also bought land between Wainui and Totaranui, including Separation Point, and areas around Awaroa River. In 1870, he entered politics by becoming a member of the House of Representatives in Wellington before retiring in 1892 and moving to Nelson, leaving his glorious estate forever. Several other families purchased the home and farm and lived in high style from the late 1800s until the economic depression of the 1930s when the pastures reverted to ferns. In 1948 the estate passed to the Crown and was incorporated in the Abel Tasman Park which had been constituted in 1942, 300 years after Tasman's visit.

Ambrose Ricketts, a shipbuilder from Nelson, purchased land at Awaroa in 1855 for its fresh water and good timber and was quickly followed by other shipwrights who moved to the well-protected bay. In just a few years, Awaroa was a well settled community with several boat-building ventures taking place. But as with Totaranui and other areas of the coast, once the main stands of timber were gone by the early 1900s, so went the shipyards and sawmills. Today only one farm remains in Awaroa, run by members of the Hadfield family, one of the original settlers.

The Wangapeka Valley remained a dark and forbidding place until gold was discovered in the Rolling, Wangapeka and Sherry rivers in the late 1850s. Dr Ferdinard von Hochstetter was believed to be the first to travel the entire route of the track when in 1860 he carried out a geological exploration trip into the valley. Quickly a pack trail was established from Nelson to the valley's eastern end for packhorses to carry supplies into the goldfields and gold out. The mining activity led to the established of the township of Bush End which was little more than a general store at the end of the cart road that was built from Nelson in 1896. The road stopped 16 km short of the Rolling River. The biggest improvement in the route came in the early 1870s when a surveyor John Rochfort cut a track along the Wangapeka River, over the saddle and down to the Karamea bed.

The nearby Heaphy also improved at the end of the century when J B Saxon surveyed and graded the track in 1888 for the Collingwood County Council. But as time passed on the sought-after gold deposits were never found and the use of both tracks declined considerably in the early 1900s. The unique flora of the area attracted visiting scientists who, among other things, reported the Heaphy's quickly deteriorating condition. They were also instrumental in setting aside Gouland Downs as a scenic reserve in 1915.

The Heaphy and Wangapeka tracks were improved dramatically in the late 1960s after the North-West Nelson State Forest Park was established in 1965 and the NZFS began to bench the routes and build huts throughout the park. But the real popularity of the Heaphy did not begin until plans for a road from Collingwood to Karamea was announced in the early 1970s. Coservationists, deeply concerned about damage to and destruction of nikau palms and other delicate flora, began an intensive campaign to stop the road and increase the usage of the track. So far they have been successful and thousands of trampers use the Heaphy each year; whether they were sucessful in stopping the road is yet to be seen.

GETTING STARTED

None of the three tracks is a circular route, and all take careful planning and usually a little busing or hitching at the end. Most trampers travelling to the area first pass through Nelson, a city where information, supplies and transportation are available. For the information go to the NZFS District Office on Harley St for anything concerning the Heaphy or the Wangapeka tracks, or to the Department of Lands and Survey (tel 81-579) for Abel Tasman National Park. These centres seem to have most of the answers and perhaps more importantly, keep regular hours, not true of all small field offices.

Headquarters for the national park is located at Takaka (tel Takaka 58026) where the chief ranger resides; a ranger can be reached at Marahau (tel Motueka 78110). There is also a visitor's centre open daily at Totaranui inside the park. For details and hiking advice for the Heaphy and Wangapeka, there are NZFS information offices in Takaka, Westport and Karamea. For information about the Wangapeka Track most trampers go to the ranger who lives 1½ km up the Dart River.

Getting to and from the tracks is a challenging even for the most experienced hikers. The Heaphy is at least a four-day trip, though most take five days, spending extra time at Heaphy Hut on the west coast. The track is best walked from the east to the west as you put the climbing behind you the first day and climax the trip with the tramp along the Tasman Sea on the final day. To get to the eastern end, jump on the Newman's bus that departs on weekdays from Nelson for Takaka and then transfer to the Collingwood Motors minibus for the final 34 km to Brown Hut. The price is reasonable when split by four or more trampers. The minibus arrives in time to take any hikers finishing back to Collingwood.

At the other end of the track there is a phone that can be used to call a taxi from Karamea Garage for the 15-km drive from Kohaihai to Karamea. A Cunningham Coach will take you from Karamea to Westport and back into civilisation. For those walking the Heaphy west to east, there is also a phone in the Brown Hut that can be used to call Collingwood Motors for a pick-up in an hour or so. The usual arrangement during the summer is for trampers to gather and be picked up by Collingwood Motors in the morning in time to connect with Newman's Takaka-Nelson run. That, of course, means spending a night at the Brown Hut.

Those with cars can arrange to meet a party walking the opposite direction and exchange keys midway through the trip. Many trampers with vehicles prefer to leave them in Collingwood as the road to Brown Hut is in very poor condition. If travelling by car from Collingwood, take the road through Rockville and Bainham where you ford two small creeks before arriving at Brown Hut. Both streams are fordable by vehicles under normal conditions. You can also hire air transport that will fly from a strip in Karamea back to the strip at Bainham, 5½ km from the Collingwood end of the track. This is a good way for a tramping party with private transport to get back to their vehicle. Arrangements should be made through Nelson

Aero Club or Nairn Air at the Nelson Airport.

The Wangapeka Track could be done in four days but due to its rough terrain, it is better to spread it out over five or more. The track is best walked east to west for easier climbs over the saddles. From Nelson, Wadsworth Motors runs a bus Monday, Wednesday and Friday that goes to Tapawera, where trampers can hire a taxi from the same company to the Dart River Ford. This puts you close to the ranger's station and an hour and a half from the east end of the track. There is no hut here but good camp-sites. If travelling from Christchurch or the West Coast, a Newmans bus passes through Kohatu, a short distance from Tapawera, and it is possible to have the Wadsworth taxi meet the bus for a trip to the Dart River. At the western end of the trail, there is a farmhouse two km down the road where you can phone for a taxi from Karamea Garage for the 26-km trip to that town. From there you can catch a Cunningham Coach bus (the same one as used by Heaphy walkers) that leaves each weekday morning for Westport, connecting you with a Newman's bus to Nelson if necessary.

If hiking in the opposite direction, trampers have to hike out to the ranger's station to make arrangements for the Wadsworth taxi to pick them up. From Tapawera, there is a Wadsworth bus that leaves for Nelson on Monday, Wednesday and Friday mornings, and on Saturday and Sunday evenings.

The Abel Tasman Coastal Track can be hiked in three days or it could be just as easy to spend five doing it. Many of the bays and inlets are worth an extra day to beachcomb for shells or explore the tidal areas for mussels or pipis. The track can be walked either direction but you should know when the tides are low. North of Anchorage Hut, Bark Bay and Awaroa are tidal flats that can easily be crossed at low tide to save from having to hike around them. If the low tide is in the morning, it is best to hike south to north, crossing the tidal areas right at the beginning of the day. If low tide is in the afternoon, then hike the other direction, covering the flats at the end of the day. Check Nelson tide tables; most huts have a copy, and then subtract 20 minutes from them. If you don't judge the tides perfectly, no need to panic. You can hike the extra distance around the bays or, if daring, roll up the pants, and wade through them; Awaroa, however, cannot be forded near high tide. My personal recommendation is to hike the trail from Marahau north, saving the scenic Separation Point as a highlight for the end.

Access to the National Park is not quite as bad as to the Heaphy. A Newman's bus from Nelson will take you to Motueka for a start from the southern end, or to Takaka for the northern end. Transport from Motueka to Marahau can be obtained with Hickmott's Motors and from Takaka to Totaranui with Bickley Motors.

Because of the generally milder and warmer temperatures of the area, especially the Abel Tasman Coast, these tracks can be undertaken from mid-October through almost the end of April or even later in some years. The

Abel Tasman Coastal Track can be walked anytime of the year; during the summer, make sure you have a swimming suit for dips in the sea, and take skin protection for the intense sun. There is also good swimming in the lagoon near the Heaphy Hut, but the Tasman Sea is generally considered too dangerous because of the strong cross currents. Raingear is important for any tramping in North-West Nelson State Forest Park, for a trip without rain would be rare.

The Abel Tasman Coastal Track is rated mild and is done often by trampers in tennis shoes. The track is wide, well marked and follows easy grades the entire trip. This combined with its coastal beauty makes it an excellent choice for those with limited or no hiking experience. The Heaphy, rated mild to medium, is well marked and benched, but has steeper climbs than Abel Tasman. What makes the Heaphy a considerably harder track than the coastal trail is the long monotonous sections of thick bush with little to look at. At times the track tends to be boring while other sections, particularly the Gouland Downs can be extremely swampy and muddy. Still, many trampers tackle the Heaphy and find the views from Perry Hut, or Mt Perry (for the adventurous), grand and the coast well worth the long walks through the bush.

The Wangapeka is the hardest walk of the three, rated medium to strenuous. The trip involves a great deal more climbing than the other two as its terrain is considerably more broken. Although the track does not have any coastal stretches, it does offer more scenic views and will have by far the least number of hikers on it during the summer.

A common practice by many trampers is to hike only park of the Abel Tasman Coastal Track or the Heaphy. A trip often done on the Abel Tasman is to walk to Anchorage Hut the first day, the Bark Bay Hut the second and then turn around and stay at the Torrent Bay Hut the third before hiking out the fourth. On the Heaphy, many simply hike up to Heaphy Hut along the West Coast then turn around, skipping the rest of the track.

The Department of Lands and Survey prints recreation maps for the Heaphy and Wangapeka tracks and another for the Abel Tasman National Park; NZMS 183. For the series one topographical maps obtain S18 and S19 for the Wangapeka, S7 and S12 for the Heaphy and S9 for the Abel Tasman Coastal Track.

ABEL TASMAN COASTAL TRACK

The coastal track is a trip that begins at the trailhead beyond Marahau and ends at Wainui Bay. For those who want to turn it into a circular trip, it is possible to hike south along the farm road from Whariwharangi Bay and pick up the Gibbs Track that ends at the Moa Park-Totaranui Track. This trail turns south through the thick bush in the western part of the park. Eventually it runs along Evans Ridge, over Moa Park and connects with Castle Rock Track. The latter runs east to Tinline Bay, a short walk from the southern trailhead. The total trip would be seven to 10 days and is

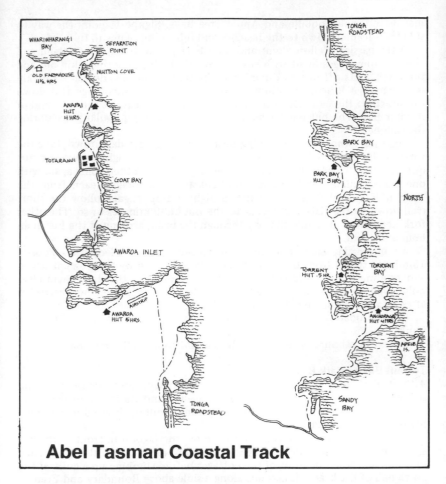

Abel Tasman Coastal Track

recommended for experienced trampers only. The western section of Abel Tasman is more difficult with much rugged terrain.

Marahau to Torrent Bay

The track begins at a turnoff one km outside Marahau on the southern end of the park. From the car park and information board, it crosses the Marahau Estuary on an all-tide causeway and then climbs gently to a clearing above Tinline Bay. There is an intentions book at the beginning of the grassy slope and another information board. The track continues around dry ridges, hugging the coast and opening up to scenic views of Adele and Fisherman Islands and Coquille and Apple Tree Bays. Signposts point the way to side trails leading down to the beaches and refreshing swims in the surf.

After passing Yellow Point and its side trail, the track turns inland and climbs along ridges lined with silver fern. At the top, the trees thin out and the track splits off in two directions. The trail to the east descends quickly to Anchorage Beach, 30 minutes away, and then to Anchorage Hut down the beach to the east. One can find glow-worms at a cave at the west end of Anchor Bay. The hut has 24 bunks and is often a very popular place during the summer.

For those who want something away from the first day crowd, take the fork to the west that leads to the Torrent Bay Hut; eight bunks and not quite as nice. This track descends towards the bay and then splits again with one trail heading for the arm that separates Anchorage Beach from the Torrent Bay tidal flats. If the tide is right, trampers can follow the short trail down to the flats and across to the hut in 30 minutes or so. The other fork heads west to circle the bay through the bush, arriving at the hut in an hour and a half.

An interesting side trail from the all-tide track is Cleopatra's Pool, a 15-minute tramp from the main track. The pool, fed by the Torrent River, is over a metre deep and surrounded by smooth rocks that lend themselves quite well to sunbathing. The cold, fresh water is a welcome refresher after a day in the sun or dips in the sea.

Accommodations: Anchorage Hut, 24 bunks; Torrent Bay Hut eight bunks.

Times: four hours to Anchorage Beach; 4½ hours to Torrent Bay.

Torrent Bay to Bark Bay

Although it's only a three-hour walk to Bark Bay, most trampers end up spending a night because of its coastal beauty and its isolation from day crowds at both ends. There is a pleasant campground, situated ideally on a bar between the beach and lagoon.

From Torrent Bay, the track skirts across the lagoon in front of the hut and south of the summer cottages. The track picks up on the other side, runs along a beach in front of the cottages before climbing up a gully at the north end of the beach. It ascends along a sidle above Boundary and Frenchman's Bays and finally breaks into the open at the top with good views of the area. It's a natural spot for a rest break. Park authorities think so — they built a bench on the side of the track for weary trampers.

The track crosses Falls River on a swing bridge and then begins a descent to Bark Bay. To reach the hut, follow the track that swings west onto an all-tide track for about 300 metres. The hut is on the south side of the trial, half hidden in bush.

Accommodation: Bark Bay Hut, 16 bunks

Time: three hours

Bark Bay to Awaroa

If the tides are cooperating, trampers can save time by cutting straight across the lagoon behind the campground to the orange marker on the other side. If not, then the all-tide track leads around the bay. From the marker, the trail ascends for half an hour to a saddle and a junction. One fork leads north-west along a bush-clad ridge to Stony Hill, over it and then down to Awaroa. The other fork is the more scenic route that sidles a swampy flat of Long Valley Creek before descending to the quarry at Tonga Roadstead. The track follows Onetahuti Beach after reaching the coast, and the granite quarry, last operated at the turn of the century, will come into full view. At the north end of Onetahuti Beach the track crosses a small tidal stream and then continues along rather soft ground, fronting the Richardson Stream Swamp. After sidling the tidal flats and the swamp, the track crosses the stream and turns abruptly north to pick up the hill route along the east side of Richardson Stream to the Tonga Saddle (260 metres). From the top of the saddle, there are good views across the Awaroa, Waiharakeke Bay, Goat Bay or even Totaranui on a clear day. The track leaves the saddle and descends to the flats of Awaroa, turns sharply west and runs alongside of an airstrip. It continues west and crosses the lagoon of Venture Creek before passing the shipwrecked hulk of the *Venture*, a 19-ton ketch that was built and buried on the shores of the same bay. From the shipwreck, it is a short walk along the shore to Awaroa Hut.

Accommodation: Awaroa Hut, 25 bunks

Time: three hours

Awaroa Hut to Anapai Hut

The Awaroa tidal area is by far the largest one crossed and trampers must pay careful attention to its condition and the current tide tables before attempting a crossing. If the tide is completely out, the two main channels will be plainly visible and it is possible to cut directly north to Pound Creek and the track for the quickest route. If not, then swing to the left in a long arc, crossing each tidal stream above its junction with the larger channels. The track ascends to a low saddle from Pound Creek, crosses over and then follows Waiharaekeke Stream back to the coast. It fords the stream and hugs the coast before spilling out into Goat Bay beach. At the north end of the beach, the track dips back into bush as it passes Skinner Point and stays in the bush until reaching an open area south of Totaranui beach.

For many trampers, their trip will be over at Totaranui where there is no hut, but good camping and some traffic to catch a ride out. Others with extra time can continue tramping around the coast for a scenic trip to Separation Point and finish at Whariwharangi Bay. For the latter, follow the road north, up the hill to its end and hike up the Anapai Bay Track, the left-hand fork at the first two junctions. The others are side trails to high points and ridges along the coast with views worth diverting for. The main track dips into a forested gully and eventually arrives at Anapai Beach with the hut a short distance to the north.

Though the hut is only 40 minutes from Totaranui, it allows trampers to spend a leisurely afternoon at Separation Point the next day or get an early start to Takaka.

Accommodation: Anapai Hut, four bunks

Time: four hours

Anapai Hut to Whariwharangi Bay

The track resumes at the north end of the beach, past the rock to little Anapai, and heads toward Mutton Cove. The terrain to Mutton Cove is mostly open country and doesn't change until the track dips to the beach at Anatakapau Bay. To reach Separation Point, follow the beach north, around rocky outcrop and along Mutton Cove. The track resumes at the north end of the second beach, climbs and follows a ridge until it breaks through the bush before the point and the lighthouse. The view from Separation Point is perhaps the most stunning of the trip. It is a sweeping scene from Farewell Spit on the horizon all the way back to Nelson on a clear day. Those who are lucky might also see members of the seal colony sunning on the rocks.

The track ends at Separation Point and trampers wishing to cut across to Whariwharangi Bay must retreat to Mutton Cove and pick up the track at the group of big pine trees. It climbs easily to the top of a ridge overlooking Separation Point and then descends to Whariwharangi Bay. At the western end of the coastal flat is an old farmhouse which has been restored as a park hut. The track behind the house runs south to the road at Wainui Inlet (two hours) and eventually to Tarakohe, the nearest village.

Accommodation: farmhouse, sleeps 10

Time: 4½ hours

HEAPHY TRACK

The following description is for walking the Heaphy east to west with most of the climbing the first day. For those who plan to hike the track west to east, more time should be allowed for ascending the spur from Lewis to MacKay and less for the walk from Perry Saddle to Brown Hut.

Brown Hut to Perry Saddle

The Brown Hut is the official beginning of the Heaphy at the east end. The hut was built to enable trampers to get an early start on the first section of the track and its steep climb. The hut holds 20 bunks but during the summer, when conditions may be become overcrowded, a few more can sleep on the floor.

The track leaves the hut, follows the Brown River for 180 metres then turns left and uses a swing bridge to cross the river. From the other side, the long haul to Gouland Downs begins as the track, now well defined, climbs

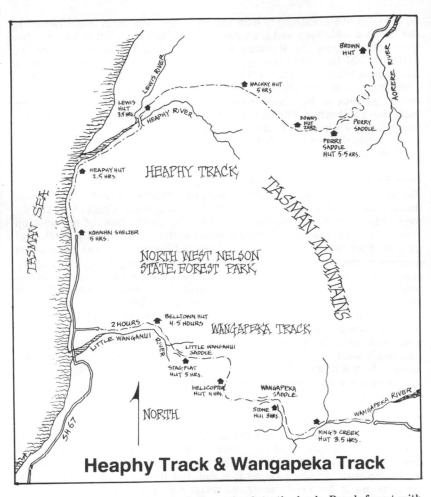

Heaphy Track & Wangapeka Track

steeply through a grass slope before moving into the bush. Beech forest with scattered podocarps and clumps of rata now surround the tramper as the track begins its monotonous switchbacks and gradual climb to the high point of 915 metres. The bush continues to be thick, views are rare and the hiking an uninspiring chore. At one point a side track descends quickly to the Aorere River and the Aorere Shelter, considered by most the halfway point to Perry Hut.

Further along the climb, trampers have an opportunity to take a well-marked shortcut that climbs the hill in a more direct route. This route saves

30 minutes but is extremely hard on the knees. The main route swings up the hill in a wide loop and is a more gradual climb even if it is longer. After about three hours the Rhubarb Shelter is reached, and after five hours of the uphill tramping, the track takes a sharp turn and begins a gentle ascent past Flanagan's Corner, the highest point of the trip at 915 metres. From here it is another 40 minutes or two km over rocky terrain and muddy tussock as the track crosses a few creeks and enters Perry Saddle with the hut nearby. The hut, 854 metres above sea level, can be a chilly spot when the wind whips through at night.

Accommodation: Perry Saddle Hut, 24 bunks
Time: six hours

Perry Saddle to Gouland Downs

The track departs from the Saddle, works its way around spurs and descends through low bush on the southern bank of the Perry Creek. Quickly the trees begin to thin out and the track opens up to the bowl of the Gouland Downs, a wide expanse of rolling tussock that is broken by patches of stunted silver beech or pygmy pine. The mud increases on the track which wanders through the often swampy Downs, first crossing Sheep Creek at the edge and then crossing a swing bridge over Cave Brook, a stream within sight of the hut. If it is January or February, mountain daisies will be in bloom along with the yellow-flowering Maori onion plant.

The Gouland Downs Hut is the oldest one on the track, well-worn and a little run down from years of constant use by trampers. It is only a two-hour walk from Perry Saddle but another five to the next hut. For those who don't want to stop at Gouland Downs or walk seven hours, one alternative is to bed down at Saxon Shelter, 2½ hours down the track.

Accommodation: Gouland Downs Hut, 13 bunks
Time: two hours

Gouland Downs to MacKay Hut

The terrain becomes level past the hut through the rest of the Downs but trampers pay the price for flat ground. The track runs through mud and then more mud and after a heavy rain it is nothing more than a quagmire of the brown stuff. In fine weather it is bad, but during a storm there is little trampers can do but keep smiling and splash right through it.

The track crosses two footbridges over Shiner Brook and Big River and then begins to climb uphill after crossing the northern fringe of the Downs. It moves back into low scrub and bush as it rises beyond Weka Stream where orange poles and mile markers dot the trail here and there. Above the stream trampers have one last look behind them at the wide expanse of the Downs and the peaks surrounding Perry Saddle before the bush closes in and the track turns into another monotonous up and down climb over several saddles. After a few boggy clearings, the track arrives at a clearing on the Saxon River where it crosses a footbridge over the stream and then passes the Saxon Shelter, a five-minute side trip.

From the emergency shelter, the track swings north and begins one final climb, regaining all the height lost in the descent to Gouland Downs. From here the first glimpse of the Tasman Sea or the mouth of the Heaphy River might be possible. The flora changes from tussock and stunted silver pine to low mountain beech and to increasingly more rata and rimu, as the track gets closer to the West Coast. The track now moves steadily downhill along a ridge, passing through a number of clearings. The final one before dense bush moves in is where MacKay Hut is situated. From the hut the views of the Tasman Sea and Gunner Downs are excellent, the sunsets on a clear night extraordinary. The mouth of the Heaphy is now only 10 km to the west.

Accommodation: MacKay Hut, sleeps 16

Time: five hours

MacKay Hut to Heaphy Hut

The track leaves MacKay Hut and returns to its muddy and boggy condition for a spell as it works steadily downhill toward the West Coast. Gradually the bush closes in along with the hills of the valley and only an occasional glimpse of the Heaphy River is possible. A hundred metres above the junction of the Lewis and Heaphy rivers, the first nikau palms pop up and are a pleasant switch in flora for trampers. The Lewis Hut, 16 bunks, is situated at the junction of the two rivers, three to four hours from MacKay Hut.

The track heads south-east after the hut for 350 metres and crosses the Heaphy on a footbridge to the south bank. It continues to follow the river bank, crossing the Gunner River and then Murray Creek on footbridges three km below the Lewis-Heaphy junction. The track passes along a stretch of river beach to the last stand of bush and then leaves the remaining hills behind and unexpectedly opens up to Heaphy Hut and then lagoon beyond. A short hike from the hut leads to the beach and the West Coast.

After struggling over much of the track, most trampers are inclined to spend a full day at Heaphy Hut. There is good swimming in the lagoon and it is possible to cross the Heaphy River at low tide and scramble through a hole in Heaphy Bluff to explore the remains of wrecked Japanese fishing boat. There is also an old trail over the bluff which can be used to visit a seal colony an hour or so up the coast. Whenever crossing the river, extreme caution must be taken.

Accommodations: Lewis Hut, 16 bunks; Heaphy Hut, 16 bunks.

Time: 6½ hours.

Heaphy Hut to Kohaihai River

Unquestionably one of the most beautiful walks in New Zealand, the final section of the track works its way south along the West Coast, always near the pounding Tasman Sea. Part of the route is along the beach where the soft sand is inviting but quickly tiring to trampers. Two-thirds of the track runs in the fringes of the beach, through the cool shade of nikau palms or works quickly up and around hill faces and small saddles. Junctions where the track leaves or returns to the beach are clearly marked.

A short distance from the hut, the track passes the Heaphy Beach Shelter and then immediately crosses a footbridge over the Wekakura Stream. After crossing a second bridge over Katipo Creek, the track passes another shelter, generally considered as the halfway point to the road's end. Still further south the track crosses a third bridge over Swan Burn and arrives at Scott's Camp where the first signs of civilisation in the form of summer cottages greet trampers. Scott's camp is a grassy clearing near the beach, just three km from the road's end and a popular spot for day hikers or families.

From the clearing, the track begins its final but very gentle climb to the saddle over Kohaihai, the end of the Heaphy Track. From the bluff, trampers return to reality as the road comes into sight and swaying palms fall into memories. A shelter with a public phone is located at the road's end.

Accommodation: Kohaihai Shelter, no bunks

Time: five hours

WANGAPEKA TRACK
The following description is for walking the Wangapeka Track from east to west with more gradual climbs over the various saddles. For those who choose to walk it in the opposite direction more time is needed from Belltown to Little Wanganui Saddle but the downhill stretch from Stag Flat to the Taipo Bridge will be faster than indicated here.

Rolling River to Stone Hut
There is a bridge near the Rolling River Shelter that crosses the river and leads the track on the south bank of the Wangapeka River. The track is well defined and the Wangepeka is almost always in sight as the trail winds in and out of bush and river flats. Any confusing sections have been well marked by the NZFS in recent years. Three hours from the start the track passes the Kiwi Log Cabin, an old hut with four bunks. The track crosses the Wangapeka here by means of a swing bridge and follows the north bank after passing a junction to a side trail up Kiwi Stream. The sign post at this point keeps trampers on the right course.

Thirty minutes further up the river, the track passes the Kings Creek Hut, a fairly new one with 30 bunks. Trampers who had to hike the extra hour and a half from the Dart River junction might want to spend the night here. Another five minutes up the track is the old King's Hut, a prospector's shelter that was built in 1935 and has four bunks. Good campsites are close to both huts.

Shortly after the prospector's hut, the track passes the junction of the North and South Branches of the Wangapeka. It continues on the north side of the North Branch through thick bush and beech forest. Half an hour before Stone Hut, the track crosses a footbridge to the south shore of the river and continues on to the hut, opposite the Stone Creek junction. Firewood can be easily gathered around a large slip 10 minutes up the track.

Accommodations: Kings Creek Hut, 30 bunks; Old Kings Hut, four bunks; Stone Hut, six bunks.

Time: six hours

Stone Hut to Helicopter Hut

The track starts in bush after leaving the hut but quickly crosses the slip, a result of the 1929 Murchison earthquake. It follows the Wangapeka River to its source and then ascends steeply up to the Wangapeka Saddle along a well marked route until reaching the top at a height of 1009 metres. At the bushclad top there is a four-way junction and a signpost pointing the way north-west over a steep and rough route to Luna Hut, south-east to a clearing on Bugget Knob, or south-west towards Helicopter Hut.

The main track leaves the saddle on a level course, crosses a small creek and then begins a rapid descent along the infant Karamea River to the valley. It crosses several side streams before working steadily along the south shore of the Karamea. The river is crossed twice not far from Helicopter Hut with easy fords if the weather is good. If not, then there is an alternative route marked with poles that continues along the south bank. The flood route takes an extra 20 minutes walking time. Both rejoin on the south bank and continue on to Helicopter Hut, just past Waters Creek. If the creek is also flooded, there is a wirewalk 30 metres upstream.

The hut has only six bunks and there is little camping in the area. The NZFS asks all trampers to avoid pitching tents on the helicopter pad.

Accommodation: Helicopter Hut, six bunks
Time: 4½ hours

Helicopter Hut to Stag Flat

The track remains on the south shore of the Karamea but begins working its way into the bush and away from the river. The track gradually climbs to Tabernacle Lookout while the Karamea carves its way through a deep and rugged gorge far below. The Tabernacle is the site of the old shelter, now gone, that was built by Jonathon Brough when he was surveying the original Wangapeka Track. The views from up here are excellent as one can see most of the Karamea Valley below.

The track leaves the lookout and after a 100 metres passes a side trail that descends steeply east to Luna Hut. The main track heads west and descends to a swing bridge across the Taipo River. On the other side of the river there is another side trail to the east which follows the Taipo past the junction with the Karamea River and finally to Trevor Carter Hut. It is possible during fair weather to hike both side trails as a round trip, adding two hours to the day's walk.

The main track follows the north bank of the Taipo and climbs gently for several km before reaching the Taipo Hut. For those who took the round trip to Trevor Carter Hut, this might be the place to stop for the night. Otherwise it is another hour and a half to Stag Flat Hut along a very steep trail. The track crosses a footbridge over Pannikin Creek 10 minutes past the Taipo Hut and then ascends steadily to Stag Flats, an area of many creeks, much bog and mud, and a lot of tussock. The hut is in good condition, has four bunks and should be used as there is poor camping in the area. The hut is situated 200 metres across the flat, south of the track.

Accommodations: Taipo Hut, 10 bunks; Stag Flat Hut, four bunks
Time: five hours

Stag Flat to Belltown Hut

The track leaves the hut and enters bush as it climbs steeply to Little Wanganui Saddle, an open clearing of snowgrass. The climb is a stiff one but the views from the top are the best of the trip. The saddle is the highest point of the track at 1087 metres and overlooks the Little Wanganui River Valley to the West Coast or back to the east at the Karamea River. The track leaves the saddle and descends quickly along a well-marked route, passing Saddle Lakes after a short time. It continues to drop steeply to the valley floor, re-entering bush and finally crossing a bridge over the little Wanganui River.

The track follows the river closely along the north bank, fording the Tangent and McHarrie creeks and then crisscrossing the Little Wanganui in the river's gorge. From here the Belltown Hut is a short distance up the north bank. A five-minute walk up the Little Wanganui brings you to a swing bridge and the new Little Wanganui Hut. Following the river through the gorge is tricky and not advisable during flooding. If the water level is high, use the route that sharply climbs over the gorge and rejoins the track downstream.

Accommodation: Belltown Hut, six bunks; Little Wanganui Hut, 16 bunks
Time: 4½ hours

Belltown Hut to Road's End

After climbs over the track's saddles, the final day to the road's end is an effortless walk for most trampers. The track is well marked and crisscrosses Little Wanganui several times as it follows the river's flats to the road's end. It fords several branches of the river and halfway down cuts through Gilmor's Clearing.

If the river is flooding, then it is necessary to climb into the bush above the north shore. This is considerably harder and doubles the walking time from Belltown Hut to the road but is unavoidable if the water is too high and swift to cross the Little Wanganui safely. Down the road 1½ km is the Stewart Homestead where there is a visitor's book and a phone that can be used to call a taxi from Karamea, 26 km away.

Time: 2½ hours.

South Island — central

Copland Track
Harper Pass
Travers-Sabine Track

When most people think of the country of New Zealand, what stands out foremost are the mountains. There are more than 70 million sheep in New Zealand, or 20 to every man, woman and child who lives there. And the Rainbow trout which were introduced at the turn of the century are today larger, purer and fiercer fighters than their ancestors in California. But more than wool sweaters and frying fillets of trout, New Zealand is mountains. The greywacke peaks, cushioned by permanent ice and snow and softened by the orange glow of the day's dying sun, are a sight long remembered after the jersey is out-grown and the last bits of trout devoured.

Vast sections of the South Island are mountainous regions that are impenetrable by most but enjoyed by all who pass by, stop and admire the grandeur of the massive landscape. The next three chapters of this book cover the backbone of the country: alpine areas of central South Island, western Otago and Fiordland. Mountain ranges run almost continuously down the middle of the island, from the Braeburn Mountains north of Nelson Lakes National Park, to the Cameron Range at the southern tip of Fiordland.

The most impressive, the mountains with a world-wide reputation among climbers, are the Southern Alps. This range stretches through the heart of the island and is protected by four national parks — Mount Cook, Westland, Arthur's Pass and Mt Aspiring — as well as a dozen state forests. Since the late 1800s mountain climbers have had an intimate relationship with the Southern Alps as they were the only ones who could travel in, out and up the rugged chain. Today there are package tours and bus rides that give visitors extraordinary views of the range.

But trampers may have the best opportunity as several tracks wind through saddles and around peaks, giving hikers a good climb and awesome scenery without requiring extensive mountaineering skills or equipment. One is the Harper Pass Track, a historical trail that begins at the Lewis Pass State Highway, cuts over the Southern Alps by way of Harper Pass and ends at SH 73.

The track begins in Lake Sumner State Forest, a 74,000-hectare preserve of beech forest, tussock grasslands, river flats and herbfields. The main divide of the Southern Alps is the western boundary of the park, joining it to Arthur's Pass National Park and allowing trampers to move across it at two saddles. Hope Pass is the lowest at 941 metres, but Harper Pass, 957 metres, has long been the most commonly used one with both gold miners and summer hikers.

The trail passes the two most accessible hot springs in the state forest before climbing over the saddle and entering Arthur's Pass National Park, a rugged and mountainous area of 98,000 hectares that straddles the main divide of the Southern Alps. Arthur's Pass is one of New Zealand's finest alpine regions. The total area above the bushline equals that below it while the park has 10 peaks rising to over 2100 metres.

A second track over the main divide is the Copland, a trail well-known in New Zealand though many Kiwis have never attempted it. The Copland is a rugged track from Mount Cook National Park, over the permanent ice and snowfields of the divide to Westland National Park. The contrast in flora and landscape is stunning as the track begins at an altitude of 745 metres at the Hermitage Hotel, climbs to 2150 at the main divide and then works down to 50 metres above sea level at the west coast.

The track takes a tramper through Mount Cook National Park, a reserve of 70,000 hectares of which one-third is permanent snow and glacial ice. It is the home of the Tasman Glacier, a flow of ice 29 km long, three km wide and one of the longest in the world outside polar regions. It is also the home of Mount Cook, New Zealand's highest mountain at 3764 metres, and 140 other peaks over 2100 metres high.

The Copland also crosses Westland National Park, a relatively new park of some 89,000 hecatres, formed in 1960. The park starts from just above sea level in lush rainforest and rises to 3300 metres, passing through tussock flats to alpine meadows and ice. Westland lies on the western side of the Southern Alps next to Mount Cook and offers the tramper its share of towering peaks and ice blue glaciers, including the famous fox and Franz Josef Glaciers.

North of the Southern Alps lies Nelson Lakes National Park, 57,000 hectares, highlighted by a pair of diamonds in Lakes Rotoiti and Rotoroa. The park has a variety of terrain that includes the flats of Travers, Sabine and D'Urville valleys and the 2000-metre peaks of Spencer Mountains, which compose the southern boundary of the reserve. Winding through the park is the circular Travers-Sabine Track that begins at Lake Rotoiti, passes along the St Arnaud Range and over the Travers Saddle to Lake Rotoroa. Although not as dramatic as Mt Cook or Arthur's Pass, Nelson Lakes offers its own alpine beauty in an area that has many trails but little traffic on them.

Weather and climate follow a general pattern through much of the central alpine regions of the South Island. North-westerlies and south-westerlies bring wind and rain off the Tasman Sea and dump most of it on the windward slopes of the Southern Alps. Trampers will find the western sections of Harper Pass and Copland tracks considerably wetter at times than the leeward sides of the trails. Rainfall ranges from 5000 mm on the windward side of Arthur's Pass and Westland, to 7500 mm at the high altitudes of the main divide, where most precipitation is in the form of snow, to 2500 mm or even less in many sections of Lake Sumner and Mt Cook. Snow may fall any time of the year down to the 1200-metre level and lies permanently at 2100 metres, making Copland Pass snow-covered much of the year.

Weather in Nelson Lakes is the exception as mountain ranges to the east and south protect the park from the effects of southerlies. North-westerlies still bring in wind and poor weather but park records show that gales are rare and conditions in the valley are calm more than two-thirds of the year. Rainfall ranges from 2500 mm in the western valleys, to 1550 mm at park headquarters in St Arnaud. Long stretches of bad weather are more likely in the spring and early summer, while spells of clear, sunny conditions are frequent in late summer and early fall.

The flora varies throughout the central region. On the eastern side of the ranges the bush is composed mainly of red, silver and mountain beech with scattered rata and broadleaf. The ground cover is thin with a light growth of ferns and sedges. On the western side the flora becomes increasingly thick due to the heavy rain dumped by westerly airstreams. You may spot massive rimu and totara along with lancewood and kamahi while the ground cover is thick with ferns and mosses.

Alpine coverage is mostly grey scree, tussock, snowgrass and, in early summer, giant mountain buttercups, known in these areas as Mt Cook lilies. In Nelson Lakes, you may find gold, green and grey vegetable sheep. From a distance this alpine plant looks like a sheep lying down with its closely-packed branches and thick leaves covering rocks like a wool jersey.

Avid bird watchers will enjoy all three tracks as the species change along with the terrain. The predominant bird is the kea, though not in numbers but rather in nature. The kea, dark olive green with scarlet feathers under the wings that are seen in flight, is an alpine parrot and has been spotted in flocks of 20 along the Copland. Naturally inquisitive of all who pass by, the kea is also found in good numbers above the bushline in Harper Pass and throughout Nelson Lakes. Also making their home in the alpine are the rock wren and the fearless New Zealand falcon. More numerous in the bush are the South Island robin, fantail, bellbird, tui, kaka, and the country's smallest bird — the rifleman. Kiwis (the birds, not the people) were once numerous and can still be sighted occasionally, particularly around the headwaters of the rivers in Lake Sumner State Forest.

Other wildlife include red deer, chamois, an occasional wild pig, hares and opossums. At Nelson Lakes, there also have been recent sightings of the country's only natural mammals, long-eared and short-eared bats, although such sightings are rare. The national park also boasts of good fishing for brown trout in Travers, D'Urville and Sabine Rivers as well as the lakes. Rainbow are found less frequently in the Sabine River and Lake

Rotoroa while Lake Sumner has good brown trout stocks in most of its rivers and lakes.

HISTORY

Maoris never settled in the central mountainous region of the South Island but the desire for greenstone pulled them over the rugged ranges in search of the precious stone on the west coast. One of their main routes was Harper Pass where they crossed the Southern Alps. The Ngaitahu of Canterbury were among the most persistent travellers as they made regular crossings for greenstone.

The Maoris were useful to the Europeans, who needed a pass from Canterbury to Westland in the mid-19th century in their quest for gold and grazing land. But it was 20-year-old Leonard Harper, with the aid of four Maori guides, who was the first European to follow the Hurunui River, cross the swampy saddle and descend the Taramakau to reach the west coast in November 1857.

It was gold that brought people and progress to Nelson Lakes. In 1860, Haast reported the discovery of gold in the Rotoiti, Rotoroa and Buller rivers, triggering a minor rush to the area. In three years a road good enough for bullock drays was built from Nelson, along the Buller River to Lake Rotoiti.

Gold did the same for Harper Pass. When gold was discovered at Greenstone in Taramakau Valley in July 1863 a lively stampede of miners, their supply trains and livestock soon followed. The route over Harper Pass became increasingly popular but it was in poor condition during the gold rush and only became worse with numerous cattle and sheep that were driven over the route to feed the miners.

With the demand for a better route, the Canterbury Provincial Government searched for an alternative pass over the main divide, and Arthur's Pass was selected. When the road was finished in the late 1860s traffic on Harper Pass slowed to a trickle and its days as the principal route were over.

Interest in the Copland Pass sparked in 1892 when the government was pushing for a route from the Hermitage to the west coast for mule traffic. Charles Douglas, explorer and surveyor, was given the task of discovering a pass and he quickly departed up the Copland River in search of it. Douglas examined several saddles and finally decided that the head of the Copland River offered the best possibilities.

Under Douglas's supervision the Copland became a regular alpine route in the 1890s with Malcolm Ross making the first west-to-east crossing of the pass in 1897 and the first women climbing it in 1903. By World War I a new track led from Hermitage to Hooker Hut with a bridge over Hooker River. On the other side a horse track was completed to Welcome Flats where there was a half-finished hut. Between the wars, traffic on the alpine route increased significantly with guided trips being offered.

After the war, the popularity of the trail faltered but picked up when Mt

Cook became a national park in 1953. Westland followed in 1960, providing the stimulus to improve the track and the huts along the route. Arthur's Pass National Park was reserved in 1929 with additional area later added to the park. Lake Sumner was established in 1969 as a State Forest Park to fully protect Harper Pass Track and Nelson Lakes was made a national park in 1956.

GETTING STARTED

Unlike other tracks grouped together with one central jumping off spot, these three are spread apart along the South Island and should be thought of separately. Harper Pass and Travers-Sabine tracks wind mostly through bush and river flats with a low alpine crossing. The Copland, however, is above the bush-line for over half its length. The trip is a true alpine crossing as the pass is snow-covered all year and ice is not uncommon, particularly in bad weather which can occur with little warning. For this reason trampers tackling the pass should have alpine equipment (such as crampons and ice axes) and the skill and experience to use it. If in doubt about your capabilities, consult the rangers at the park headquarters, or perhaps hire a guide. Other gear should include glacier goggles, gaitors and snow cream.

The track can be walked from either direction but most trampers go from east to west, preferring to start at 750 metres rather than sea level and making the ascent to the pass quickly instead of gradually climbing from the west coast. Also the hot springs at Welcome Flats seem to be enjoyed more after the crossing when the muscles are recovering from the steep climb.

If crossing the pass from east to west, Mt Cook Village is the place to outfit the trip. Although food supplies might be limited, the service centre is where you can rent mountaineering equipment, hire guides and obtain information. The Mt Cook National Park headquarters, down the road from the THC hotel, will supply the latter and assist you in any way in organising an expedition across the pass.

Don't let the lack of mountaineering skills prevent you from crossing New Zealand's best alpine pass. From Alpine Guides Ltd, located at Mt Cook Village, you can obtain the needed equipment and a guide who will meet you at Hooker Hut and take your party over the pass to the head of the Copland Valley. Afterwards he will carry the axes and ropes back with him, thus lightening your load.

For transport to Mt Cook Village, the Mt Cook Lines bus service takes you right to the door of the park headquarters. Along SH 6, there is a regular NZRRS bus service between Haast and Fox and more frequent runs north of Fox to Hokitika and Greymouth. The only problem is that Fox is 27 km north of the trailhead on the west coast. It is sometimes possible to arrange for the NZRRS buses to make pick-ups at trailheads though it is not a common practice on every track. Hitching is good during the height of the summer but any other time it is known to be slow.

It is best to arrive at Mt Cook Village in the morning and begin hiking that day, since it is only a three-hour walk to Hooker Hut. Lodging at the tourist centre tends to be expensive and camping at White Horse Hill can be unattractive. The huts along the track are controlled by Mt Cook or Westland National Parks and users are charged a fee for overnight use. Most are well-equipped with gas burners or wood stoves, an assortment of pots and pans and a two-way radio linked to the Mt Cook or Westland networks. Each night after 7 pm there is a weather report for the next day followed by each hut calling in its hiking plans. There is something adventurous about the hut reports as you listen to the crackled voices of trampers giving names and bits of information from all around the parks.

A popular trip for many who want to avoid the high alpine section of the Copland is to hike in from the west coast, spending the first night at Welcome Flats, a 5½-hour hike from the road. On the second day you could hike to Douglas Rock Hut and beyond above the bushline before returning to Welcome Flats, and on the third day hike back out to SH 6. This trip can be done without any special skills.

St Arnaud, a small town located at the head of Lake Rotoiti, is the site of the park headquarters for Nelson Lakes and the jumping off spot for most trips into the area. The town is connected with Nelson by Wadsworth Motors which make three runs a week to the park on Monday, Wednesday and Friday. Accommodation in the area includes camp grounds, motor camp, motels and Rotoiti and Red Deer Lodge, large bunk huts.

The Travers-Sabine Track is a near circular five-day route that can begin and end at St Arnaud for those with their own transport. On the final day of the trip at Lake Rotoroa, you can hike back to St Arnaud, down the lake to Rotoroa or arrange for a boat pick-up and cruise to the north end of Lake Rotoroa. Inquire at the park headquarters about available boat charters.

Harper Pass and Copland require special planning to return to a car parked at one end. For the Copland, the return could involve either a lenthy bus trip back to Mt Cook Village, or an air charter out of Fox. From the end of Harper Pass at SH 73, both bus and train are available for the trip back to Lake Sumner. The track for the five-day Harper Pass trip begins at a car park and bus shelter on SH 7, 48 km south of Springs Junction or 162 km north of Christchurch. The track passes into Arthur's Pass National Park

A Tidal flats at the beginning of the Abel Tasman Coastal
   Track
B Ferns on the Heaphy Track
C The weka, flightless bird found throughout the South
   Island

and ends near Aickens, where there are public phones, a bus stop and a rail station. From Aickens, you can take the train west to Greymouth or east to Arthur's Pass. There is also a NZRRS bus service in both directions from Aickens, Monday through Friday. It is possible to leave a vehicle at Hanmer Springs, hike the trail and bus back to the car.

Those without private transport may find it easier on the Copland and Harper Pass as there will be no need to return to the beginning of the track.

All three tracks involve an alpine crossing and considerable climbing. They are rated strenuous for the Copland and medium to strenuous for Travers-Sabine and Harper Pass. Hikers should not be discouraged from undertaking them; just be prepared physically for the invigorating exercise on the trails. It is essential on these trips to take warm clothing such as a woollen hat and mittens and on the Copland, woollen trousers. None of the trips is longer than five days but you still might consider investing in some freeze-dried food to keep the pack as light as possible for the uphill climb.

The Nelson Lakes recreation map covers the entire Travers-Sabine Track or you can purchase series one topographical maps S33 and S40. For Harper Pass, carry topographical maps S53 and S52. For the Copland, use either the Westland and Mt Cook recreation maps or series one topographical S79.

COPLAND TRACK
The following description is a four-day trip from Mt Cook Village to SH 6 with nights spent at Hooker Hut, Douglas Rock and Welcome Flats. To save a day, you can push on from Hooker Hut to Welcome Flats and out on the third day, skipping a night at Douglas Rock.

Mt Cook Village to Hooker Hut
The track begins beyond the Hermitage, next to the memorial dedicated to the first climbers to die on Mt Cook. It winds through small moraine hills along Hooker River and quickly moves into sight of Mt Cook. Bit by bit the massive mountain shows its south face and eventually fills the entire view from the valley. The track crosses the Hooker River twice on swing bridges and at times skirts high above the stream on wooden platforms.

Leaving the bridges, the track wanders through flats and terraces where

A The Routeburn Valley, seen from the Routeburn Falls Hut
B The Routeburn Falls Hut and the Routeburn Valley below

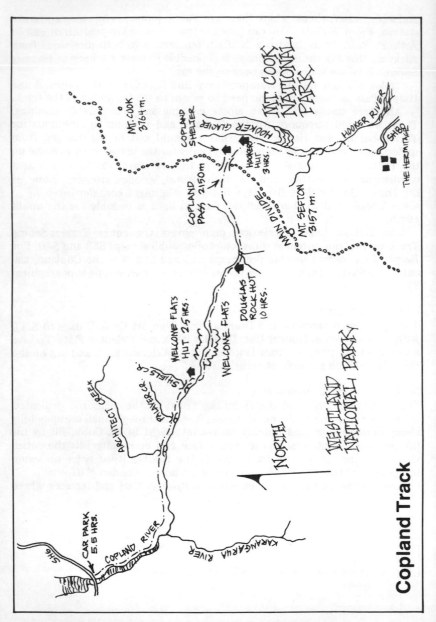

Copland Track

you should see plenty of alpine flora. In early summer wildflowers are in bloom with Mt Cook lily outshining them all. Gradually the track crosses Stocking Steam and arrives at the lunch shelter on the other side. Beyond the shelter, the track begins its steep climb through a landscape of brown buttresses, bare rock outcrops and hanging ice.

The route arrives unexpectedly at the crest of a moraine where the Hooker Glacier can be viewed to the east. Although slowly melting away now, at one time the glacier was 240 metres thick and extended several km down the valley. The track descends from the moraine and crosses several unbridged streams and gullies. It then makes its final climb along a series of switchbacks through alpine scrub to a terrace that is followed until Hooker Hut is reached, 10 km uphill from the Hermitage.

Accommodation: Hooker Hut, 12 bunks

Time: three hours

Hooker Hut to Douglas Rock

From Hooker Hut, the route is marked by orange posts and cairns for a short distance. Trampers should be aware of this and be extra alert to follow the correct route over the pass. The route climbs high before entering the first gully above the hut and then crosses it. This gully is exposed to avalanches so take care when crossing it. Marked poles point the way across the face of two small ridges and a shallow dip before leading up the main ridge to Copland Pass. It is best to stay with the crest of the ridge, bypassing snow slopes and gullies on the side.

The route now climbs up and along the ridge, and is relatively easy to follow when the snow has melted. It bears left over a snowgrass slope and climbs a bluff which can be avoided by staying left on the shingle slopes. The route returns to the ridge for a scrambling ascent to the metal emergency shelter. The silver barrel hut is a good place to take a rest as the three hours from Hooker Hut are the hardest climb of the day.

The shelter is located on the foot of the main snow slope and the route continues on to the slope after leaving the emergency hut. It swings right at the top of the snow slope, rounds a crevasse and in less than an hour from the shelter, arrives at the main divide on the Copland Pass, 2150 metres above sea level. The view from the 'roof of New Zealand' is immense if the weather is clear. To the south is the Tasman Valley, to the west one might see the Tasman Sea and all around are the peaks of the Southern Alps, dwarfed by Mt Cook's overpowering size.

The pass is no place to linger, however, as clouds can suddenly blow up from Westland, smothering the view and causing undue panic among those who fear losing the route. The pass is best crossed to the south along a steep and narrow gully. The gully descends 50 metres and the route leaves it and sidetracks for a spell to snow and scree basins. In the lower basins on the left, the route resumes again and wanders through tussock to broken terrain and a waterfall. From here, it follows a series of switchbacks to the head of the Copland Valley and continues to descend to the bushline, located at the first bend in the river.

Three small gullies and their mountain streams are crossed before the track reaches the south side of the Copland Valley and becomes well defined and maintained again. After a short distance into the forest, the track passes Douglas Rock Hut, a welcome sight after a long day over the pass.

Accommodation: Douglas Rock Hut, 12 bunks
Time: 10 hours

Douglas Rock to Welcome Flats

After the hard day over the Copland, most trampers look forward to the short, pleasant hike to Welcome Flats Hut and especially the hot springs waiting for them. A good track leaves the hut, crosses a swing bridge over a stream and works its way through forest around a ridge. It follows the broken Copland River and at one point ascends an overgrown slip.

From here it drops into Welcome Flats, a pleasant tussock clearing along the river surrounded by peaks and snowfields. On a clear day, it is hard not to justify an extended break in this area to contemplate the scenery or to gather one's thoughts. The track continues on the west side of the flats, marked by rock cairns at the beginning of the bush. It works quickly through the bush and in 30 minutes from the flats, trampers arrive at the huge swing bridge and the hot springs are a hop, skip and a jump from the hut.

There are actually three separate pools at the springs. The first is the hottest as the water comes into it directly from the ground. Most bathers prefer the second pool with the third, the last to catch the steaming water, usually too cool. A midnight soak on a clear evening is a highlight of the trip as weary hikers lie back in the naturally heated water and count the falling stars streaking across the sky.

Accommodation: Welcome Flats Hut, 16 bunks.
Time: 2½ hours.

Welcome Flats to SH 6 Car Park

From the hut, thick bush of rimu and totara surround the track all the way to the cattle grazing flats at the end. The trail is well marked and benched, and stays high above the river as it drops steadily into the valley It crosses a handful of streams and two of them, Shields and Palaver, have footbridges that should be used during flooding.

After dropping 300 metres from Welcome Flats Hut, the track crosses Architect Creek over a swing bridge. The track swings towards the river's edge after crossing Architect and follows the Copland shore, forcing trampers to hop from one large boulder to another. Be careful in this stretch as the footing is extremely slippery when wet. The river's edge is followed for a stretch before an orange marker directs trampers back into the bush.

Once back in lush rain forest, the track climbs up and away from the Copland.

The trail now appears wide in many stretches, a result of the old horse track that once ran through to Welcome Flats Hut. Eventually it arrives at a side trail that leads off to a good view of the junction of the Copland and Karangarua Rivers. The track continues its easy grade through the thick forest until it breaks out of the bush onto the flats at the end where a few head of cattle eye all who pass by.

Once in the flats, orange posts guide trampers across the grazing land to Rough Creek, a stream that has to be forded twice before reaching the parking lot at the head of the trail.

Time: 5½ hours

TRAVERS-SABINE TRACK
This is a five-day trek from St Arnaud to Rotoroa and includes walking the length of both Lake Rotoiti and Lake Rotoroa. The trip can also be turned into a circular route by hiking from Sabine Hut on the fifth day through Howard State Forest on the Howard Track and then cutting back to St Arnaud by way of Speargrass Track to the Mt Robert road and SH 63.

St Arnaud to Lake Head Hut
From the park headquarters, the road leads to the trailhead on the eastern side of Lake Rotoiti, opposite the peninsula. The track travels through beech forest but it always stays close to the lake shore to the head of Rotoiti. There are views of the lake to the west and glimpses of the St Arnaud Range as you work your way south around the lake.

After crossing four side streams, the track runs through a stand of rimu. The native tree is easy to identify by its dark brown bark, which flakes off in large scales leaving a wavy pattern on the trunk. This stand is the only one known in the Lake Rotoiti watershed and is at the greatest altitude they are known to grow in the park. The rest of the forest is composed of silver, red and mountain beech.

At the head of Rotoiti, the track leaves the lakeside and travels a short distance up the Travers River Flats to Lake Head Hut. If the river is low, one can easily ford it and also Coldwater Stream on the far side of the flat to reach Coldwater Hut and the Travers Track. For those with an early start start and extra energy, it is five hours to the next hut if you want to cut out an extra day.

Accommodation: Lake Head Hut, 16 bunks; Coldwater Hut, six bunks.
Time: 2½ hours to Lake Head; three hours to Coldwater.

Lake Head Hut to Upper Travers Hut
From Lake Head Hut, hike south along the Travers Track which follows the east bank of the river before crossing a swing bridge to the west bank, an hour and a half from Lake Head Hut.

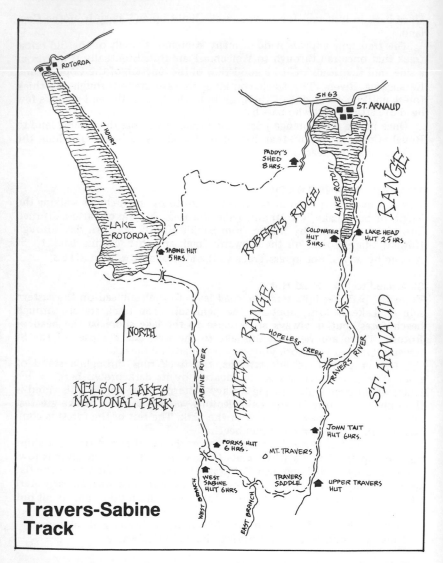

Travers-Sabine Track

An alternative is to ford the Travers River and Coldwater Stream to reach the track on the western side. This track is easier walking, but hardly makes up the time lost in crossing the valley flat.

For three km from Coldwater Hut the valley is broad and flat, a reminder

For three km from Coldwater Hut the valley is broad and flat, a reminder of the early sheep stations that used the land for grazing. The track winds through the valley and crosses Shift Creek before arriving at the junction with Cascade Track, a side trail that leads west up the Hikere Stream to Lake Angelus in the Travers Range. Shortly after this junction, the track passes the footbridge and joins the trail from the Lake Head Hut.

The track gradually swings south-west and opens up to a scenic view of Mt Travers while working its way towards Hopeless Creek and the side trail to Hopeless Hut. Hopeless Creek can be forded in normal conditions but there is a footbridge a few metres upstream in case of flooding. The track continues on the west bank but climbs at one point to swing around a gorge. Two hours from Hopeless Creek, the track arrives at a footbridge, crosses it and reaches John Tait Hut on the other side of the stream.

About 10 minutes after leaving the hut, the track passes the junction to Cupola Hut, and crosses the footbridge over Cupola Stream immediately afterwards. From here the track climbs steadily, crossing a footbridge over Summit Creek within an hour. Halfway to Upper Travers Hut, it switches to the east bank of the river over another footbridge and keeps climbing out of the valley to avoid the rough travel on the valley floor. The Upper Travers Hut, under the flanks of Mt Travers, appears in the last stand of beech on the bushline, three hours from John Tait Hut.

Accommodation: John Tait Hut, 16 bunks; Upper Travers Hut, 16 bunks.
Time: four hours to John Tait Hut; seven hours to Upper Sabine Hut.

Upper Travers Hut & West Sabine Hut

From the hut, trampers climb to Travers Saddle which crosses the range south of Mt Travers and leads into the valley formed by the East Branch of the Sabine River. At the hut the track crosses to the west bank of the river on a footbridge only two km from its source. It climbs south-west above the bushline over snow-grass and scree to a terrace under the south ridge of the mountain.

The track over the ridge becomes a route but is clearly marked by metal standards. It makes its way over the saddle and then descends the steep western slope of snowgrass and scree to the bush edge. Gradually the track veers north-west to a shingle gully and then follows it sharply down to the bushline and the Sabine River. The descent is rapid and trampers should be cautious during and after heavy rain. From the saddle, the track drops 780 metres to the river where it crosses a foot bridge over a spectacular gorge carved out by the East Branch.

The track follows the East Branch until it arrives at the river's fork. Here are two footbridges with one leading north to the nearby Forks Hut and the other west to cross the river to the Sabine Track. There is also a short side trail south to the West Sabine Hut.

Accommodations: Forks Hut, eight bunks; West Sabine Hut, eight bunks.
Time: six hours

Forks Hut to Sabine Hut

From the Forks Hut, cross both footbridges to pick up the track on the west bank of the Sabine River. The track runs along the west bank for almost the entire valley and tramping is relatively easy in this section of the park.

Four hours from the hut, the track leaves the river's side briefly to avoid a deep gorge. It quickly returns to the Sabine and 30 minutes past the gorge it arrives at a track junction and a footbridge. The side trail to the west heads around the head of Lake Rotoroa and eventually to D'Urville Hut. The footbridge leads to the Sabine Hut Trail, two km or 30 minutes down the track on the eastern shore of the lake.

Accommodation: Sabine Hut, 16 bunks

Time: five hours

Sabine Hut to Rotoroa or St Arnaud

From the Sabine Hut, there are three methods of returning to civilisation. First there is the Lake Rotoroa Track that runs along the eastern shore of the lake. The track is a difficult one as it crosses a lot of small ridges and gullies for a tiring hike. It ends up at the Rotoroa campground after 18 km and seven hours of hiking from the hut. At Rotoroa there is a ranger station and in the summer enough traffic to pick up a ride back to the main highway or St Arnaud.

The second alternative is to head north-east on the Howard Track through the Howard State Forest. The track crosses the Tier Stream several times before arriving at a derelict NZFS hut. From here the Speargrass Track leads off to the east, cutting across the state forest to Speargrass Hut, another NZFS hut on the border of Nelson Lakes National Park. The track continues along Speargrass Creek and finally veers north-west to climb to Mt Robert Shelter which is located on a road that leads back to SH 63 and eventually St Arnaud. One option for hikers with their own transport is to park the car near the shelter and begin tramping the first day on the Travers Track that runs along the western shore of Lake Rotoiti to Coldwater Hut.

The third alternative from Sabine Hut is to arrange for a boat lift from the wharf close to Sabine Hut. Check the park board headquarters in St Arnaud for information and arrangements on such charters.

Time: seven hours to Rotoroa; eight hours to Mt Robert carpark.

HARPER PASS TRACK

This is a five-day trip over Harper Pass from Lake Sumner State Forest to Arthur's Pass National Park beginning on the north bank of the Hope River. The track is relatively new and parts of it are not shown on the topographical series one map S53. Trampers planning to hike the track should obtain a trail map from the Forest Service office in Hanmer Springs or Christchurch.

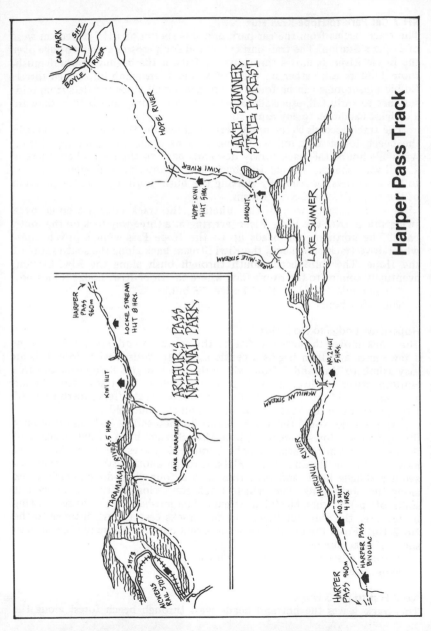

Harper Pass Track

SH 7 Car Park to Hope-Kiwi Hut

The track begins from the car park and bus shelter on SH 7, three km west of Poplars Station. The trail darts west and soon crosses a swing bridge over the Boyle River. It moves through river flats at the beginning where mushroom hunters can gather up their prey and then climb into beech forest. Edible mushrooms can be found in abundance all along the flats from midsummer to early fall, especially after a shower. Plump and tender, they are a delicious addition to any camp stew.

The track ascends to the upper terrace above the Hope River and stays in the beech forest as it follows the north bank along a well-developed trail. After 2½ hours, the track slowly descends back to the river where there is a half-way shelter, leaving the bush and re-entering wide-open flats. It follows the flats, occasionally skirting the bush, until it passes the junction of the Hope River and Kiwi Stream.

A short distance west of the junction, the track crosses a gorge by a swing bridge over the Hope River, arriving at a three-way fork on the south bank. The northern trail heads up to the Hope Pass while a private four-wheel-drive track cuts across the Kiwi Stream back along the south shore of the Hope. The third heads south through bush along the Kiwi Stream, eventually coming to the river's flats where the Hope-Kiwi Lodge is located.

Accommodation: Hope-Kiwi Lodge, 18 bunks

Time: five hours.

Hope-Kiwi Lodge to No 2 Hut

The track moves through the flat to the southern end, crosses the stream a few times and then begins a gentle ascent towards Kiwi Saddle. It is an easy climb to the saddle, from where the track begins its descent towards Hurunui River. A short distance from the saddle, the track comes to the junction of a side trail which leads to a lookout that offers superb views of Lake Sumner and the Brothers Mountains on the south side.

After the lookout, the track begins to descend a little more rapidly through beech forest, crosses Three-Mile Stream by a swing bridge and finally emerges at the head of Lake Sumner. It leaves the beech forest and moves onto the Hurunui River Flats, through another stretch of beech to avoid a shingle bluff, and then runs into a four-wheel-drive vehicle track along the north bank. The vehicle track stays close to the bush edge but splits off a km from McMillan Stream. The left-hand fork crosses a swing bridge over the Hurunui River and backtracks east a short distance to the No 2 Hut. From the hut there is a track that continues around the southern shore of Lake Sumner.

Accommodation: No 2 Hut, 18 bunks.

Time: five hours.

No 2 Hut to No 3 Hut

The track leaves the hut and heads west through beech forest along the south shore of the Hurunui River. Two km from the hut it breaks out into river flats again and stays in this terrain until it passes the junction of the track to Mackenzie Stream. The track passes two hot springs shortly after the junction and ascends to a bush terrace before dipping down to the flats again.

The track follows the flats with the bush close at hand. It runs into a vehicle track on the south bank and follows it for the next 20 minutes until it reaches No 3 Hut. If the four-hour hike from No 2 Hut isn't quite enough, it is another hour along the vehicle track through bush and river flats to the Cameron Hut, a small shelter that sleeps only four.

Accommodation: No 3 Hut, 16 bunks; Cameron Hut, four bunks.

Time: four hours.

No 3 Hut to Locke Stream Hut
From No 3 Hut, the track remains on the south shore of the river, winding through bush and river flats for 30 minutes, before reaching the walkwire across Cameron Stream. An hour from the hut, the track passes Cameron Hut and then gradually works its way back into the bush and away from river flats.

The Hurunui now turns into a mountain stream and the track begins its steady climb toward Harper Pass, two hours beyond Cameron Hut. It crosses a small stream and reaches a bivouac that sleeps two before beginning a steeper ascent to Harper Pass (960 metres). The trail to the pass is well defined as it follows the south bank of the Hurunui River, fords it one last time and in 30 minutes climbs sharply to the top. Trampers in good hiking condition will have few problems with it except in adverse weather, in which case it's better to postpone the crossing.

The pass offers good views but is not a place to linger as it is rather exposed. The track descends from the saddle and quickly comes to the north bank of the Taramakau River, one km from its source. For the next hour, it swings away from the stream and descends sharply towards the valley. This part of the track can be extremely rough and trampers should take their time so as not to lose the trail markings along the way. After an hour or so, the track crosses back over to the south shore over a footbridge and from there becomes a mixture of track and route. Both follow the river-bed and trampers should have few problems making their way along the marked section to Locke Stream Hut, located past the first clearing and before Locke Stream. The hut is a three-hour tramp from the saddle and is controlled by Arthur's Pass National Park which charges a fee for its use.

Accommodation: Harper Pass Bivouac, sleeps two; Locke Stream Hut, 18 bunks.

Time: seven hours from No 3 Hut.

Locke Stream to SH 73
The track leaves the hut, skirts through some bush and then quickly emerges

on the open river flats again. Most trampers simply follow the river for the remainder of the trip unless high water dictates otherwise. Several fords of small streams or branches of the Taramakau might be necessary if following the river. In 3½ hours the track passes Kiwi Hut (six bunks) in a clearing on the north shore of the river.

The track passes the hut by and in less than two km reaches a junction with the side trail up the Otehake River. If flooding has occurred on the Taramakau, this is an alternative route: it heads safely on the Otehake, across a footbridge and then swings north-west around Lake Kaurapataka back to the main track. This walk would take an hour and a half.

The main track continues on the open river flats until it moves through an arm of bush and comes to another trail junction. The left-hand fork leads south along a branch of the Taramakau for an hour and a half before crossing a footbridge to the railroad tracks and SH 73. The right-hand fork fords the same channel, moves through bush and shortly arrives at the Aickens Post Office and bus stop on the side of SH 73. The rail stop is just a short distance south on the highway.

Time: 6½ hours

South Island — Mt Aspiring

Routeburn Track
Rees-Dart Track
Greenstone-Caples Track

When you look up there is snow, ice and bare mountain peaks. When you look down the scene changes to wide tussock flats, dense beech forest, fast-moving rivers and a mist that is moving in to cover it all. Mt Aspiring National Park is set in wide river valleys and secluded flats, encased by mountain ranges, encrusted by more than 50 glaciers and topped by peaks of over 2700 metres.

Here is a nugget of alpine gold. With its rugged beauty of sheer-sided mountains, this part of western Otago is a fitting end to the world-renowned Southern Alps. Its rainforest bush is also a proper introduction to neighbouring Fiordland while its glaciers, hanging valleys and snow-capped peaks give it a character all its own.

The contrast of hiking from dry beech forest to alpine meadows to rain forest has appealed to trampers for years and led to a quick development of tracks and huts throughout the area. Three of the oldest and best-known trails are the heavily used Routeburn, Rees-Dart and Greenstone-Caples. All lie either partly in or next to Mt Aspiring National Park, a reserve of 287,000 hectares between the Milford and Haast highways. The park is the source for seven major rivers, the home of Mt Aspiring (3027 metres) and a region that is crisscrossed by a dozen mountain ranges.

The Rees and Dart rivers, which both drain into the head of Lake Wakatipu, are generally regarded as the best round-trip in the park. The two rivers separate the Forbes Mountains from the Southern Alps on the west and the Richardson Range on the east and are linked together by the Rees Saddle, the low point of 1450 metres between them. The Rees, protected from westerlies by the Forbes, has a drier, warmer climate which accounts for its forest of mountain beech. It also produces the valley's claim for the best tramping weather in the region. The Dart is colder and wetter and is composed of red beech in the lower reaches and silver beech in the upper portions of the river. The bush is considerably thicker than that found along the Rees while the terrain is steeper with a lack of wide open tussock flats and grassland.

Rainfall varies with the upper portion of the Dart receiving as much as 5000 mm annually and the Lower Rees as little as 1500 mm. Winds can come out of the north-west, last several days and usually bring rain or mist with moderate temperatures; the front will then usually switch to a southerly, a clearing wind that gives rise to better weather. The common weather pattern for the river valleys during the summer is for one or two days of stormy north-west winds followed by a swing to south or south-west with a sharp drop in temperatures and clear conditions.

Birdlife is plentiful along both rivers with New Zealand pigeons, fantails, paradise and gray ducks, pukeko and tuis being the most abundant species. Other wildlife that might be sighted are red and Virginian deer, chamois, opossums, and occasionally a goat, a descendant from those that escaped the heavy workloads of goldminers at the turn of the century.

At the tip of the national park is the Routeburn, unquestionably the best known and most heavily used track in western Otago. The Routeburn is a three-day passage across the Main Divide that connects the Eglinton and lower portion of the Dart valleys. Like the Dart, it has thick, rain-forested bush with red, mountain and silver beech forming the canopy, and ferns, mosses and fungi covering everything below like wall-to-wall shag carpet.

But it is the subalpine sections of the track that have been so appealing to trampers over the years. The tranquility of a tussock meadow, sprinkled with giant buttercup and flowering spaniard, and the dramatic views of entire valleys or mountain ranges is ample reward for the extra encounters with other hikers going both ways. As you take the final steps past Harris Saddle, the entire Hollyford Valley, from Gunn's Camp right to Martins Bay, opens up at your feet. At Key Summit, a short hike from the Lake Howden Hut, the view not only includes the Hollyford, but the Greenstone and the Eglinton valleys as well.

The track is highly developed and well maintained to cope with almost 7000 hikers who enjoy the Routeburn every year. The huts tend to be new, large and almost too comfortable, especially the one at Lake Mackenzie. Those who like the feeling and adventure of an unboarded and undeveloped track would prefer the Rees-Dart or the Greenstone-Caples over the Routeburn, which at times may resemble an international border crossing.

The Routeburn has the same hearty birdlife as the Rees-Dart, but with a more noticeable number of keas, or mountain parrots, in the alpine areas. Most trampers meet their first kea at Routeburn Falls where two or three hut birds hang out. Their personality and curiosity will capture your heart and fancy. They will sit on the edge of the roof, twist their heads 180° over the side and watch trampers inside for the entire dinner hour. In the morning or after a fresh snow, they can be seen sliding down the tin roof. They will walk within a few cm for a better look at a resting hiker or his backpack.

They will be enjoyed, but they also should be watched with a close eye. Keas like to steal anything shiny. Rings, watches compasses in a metal case and tin cups have been known to disappear in a wink of the eye. The birds also delight in tearing things apart — backpacks, hiking boots or even (as one unlucky tramper told me) a brand new goose-down sleeping bag still in its stuff sack. The powerful beak is capable of ripping into shreds just about anything carried in a backpack. Keas are also capable of picking up large sticks and banging a drum roll on the hut roof at ungodly hours in the morning. Suddenly, keas are not so cute anymore.

The mountain environment not only produces many encounters with the fun-loving keas but also rainfalls up to 5000 mm per year and a possibility of snow to the 1000-metre level any month. Like the Rees-Dart, winds are north-west or south-west and exceptionally strong at times on the exposed western face between Harris Saddle and Lake Mackenzie. This is one stretch of the track that should not be crossed in foul weather. An extra day's wait at Routeburn Falls for good weather is well worth the panorama obtained on a clear day.

The third track in western Otago, but not in Mt Aspiring Park itself, is the Greenstone-Caples, a three-day hike around the Ailsa Mountains in Wakatipu State Forest. The Greenstone portion is an old trail which was for years the only means of getting back to Lake Wakatipu from the Routeburn. The track runs from Lake Howden to Elfin Bay along the board-flat valley of the Greenstone River.

The Caples track has been developed and improved in the past few years, making it a well-defined track up the valley and over the lower saddle to the Greenstone on the eastern side of Lake McKellar. For many the track is an alternative to the crowded summer conditions of the Routeburn, making it increasingly popular every year.

Although not as dramatic as the Routeburn nor possessing as much rugged mountain scenery as the Rees-Dart, the circular track offers its own beauty in the wide-open tussock flats of the Greenstone River or the beech forest and grass clearing of the Caples. Most trampers prefer the Caples Valley, finding it much more attractive than the Greenstone although it is a steeper and harder hike.

Weather follows the same pattern as the other two tracks with winds coming out of the north-west and south-west and a heavy rainfall most of the year. The Caples Valley tends to be a little drier and more pleasant than the Greenstone.

HISTORY

There are traces of a village at the mouth of the Routeburn and a moa-hunting site near Glenorchy, but the real value of this area to the Maoris was its use as a trade route between South Westland and Central Otago. The first people wandered through in search of moas in the mid-1300s and possibly even settled portions of the Routeburn, lower Dart and Rees valleys. But when the giant bird became extinct in about 1500 the native population moved back to the coast for food.

The Routeburn and Greenstone valleys were still important, however, as they were a crucial link for Maoris securing greenstone from both the west coast and the Routeburn area. Greenstone expeditions are said to have been held as late as 1850 — about the same time the first Europeans began poking around the region without the aid of any maps.

Much of the veil of obscurity over the upper Wakatipu area was first lifted by W G Rees. After establishing his sheep station near Queenstown in 1860, he sailed to the head of Lake Wakatipu in September of that year and discovered the Rees and Dart rivers draining into it. In 1861, he set up a sheep station near Glenorchy and was granted the lower flats of the Rees for stocking. In the same year, David McKellar and George Gunn, part explorers and part runholders, shed some light on Greenstone Valley when they struggled up the river and then climbed one of the peaks near Lake Howden. What they saw was the entire Hollyford Valley, but they thought they were looking at the George Sound in Fiordland. The great Otago gold rush began later that year and by 1862 prospectors were shifting the soil around the lower regions of the Dart and Rees as well as the Routeburn Valley.

Explorer and prospector Patrick Caples made a solo journey up the Greenstone from Lake Wakatipu in 1863 and then discovered the Harris Saddle before descending into the Hollyford Valley and out to Martins Bay. Caples, brave enough to cross the Ailsa Mountains on his own, saw a native hut near the beach in Martins Bay and smoke from a fire and panicked back into the bush, afraid to approach the handful of Maoris despite his starving condition.

James Hector, chief geologist for the Provincial Government of Otago, unknowingly followed Caples footsteps later in 1863, searching for a route to build a road to the west coast. But the plan for the road and settlement in Martins Bay never succeeded as a harsh west coast environment and a jealous Dunedin business community, not wanting the gold from Otago to go to Australian bankers, foiled the attempt.

Miners were mystified by the hidden valleys and streams of the area, dreaming of a mother lode that was yet to be discovered, but little evidence of gold was found and the miners began to look towards the west coast and Hokitika for new strikes.

While much exploration and prospecting was done in the Humboldt Mountains, the Olivines and Rees Valley, little was undertaken in the upper portion of the Dart. The first person to cross the Barrier Range from Cattle Flat in the Dart to a tributary of the Arawata River was William O'Leary, better known as Arawata Bill. The long-time prospector roamed the mountains and valleys of this area and much of the Hollyford River for 50 years, searching out various minerals and enjoying the solitude of open and desolate places. Unfortunately, Arawata Bill kept most of his information about passes and routes he discovered to himself.

Mountaineering and a thriving local tourist industry began developing in the late 1890s and was booming, even by today's standards, in the early 20th century throughout the Mt Aspiring area. Richard Bryant of Kinloch and Birley of Glenorchy took visitors on horseback to the Routeburn Flats and on the following day led them up the Harris Saddle for the view. There was also much interest and activity round the Rees, which was served by several hotels in Glenorchy and guiding companies which advertised trips up the valley by horse and buggy.

The Routeburn was completed to Lake Howden when Sir Thomas Mackenzie, Minister of Tourism, pushed for its construction by getting Birley to search out for a route in 1912. Birley discovered Lake Mackenzie and a year later work began to carve out a track along the Hollyford face. It was finished by the outbreak of World War I. The final section of the trail was built in the late 1930s when the road toward Milford Sound from Te Anau was completed by relief workers during the Depression. Until then a tramp on the Routeburn meant returning on the Greenstone.

Relief workers also cut a stretch of the Rees-Dart Track when they carved out a horse route from Cattle Flat to the junction of the Dart and Snowy Creek. The final five km to the Dart Hut was constructed in 1939 by contract workers, finally connecting both river tracks. By 1945 the round trip had become a popular tramp, second only to the Routeburn in the Mt Aspiring area.

The first action to make Mt Aspiring a national park came in 1935, but it was not until 1964 that the government formally preserved the natural beauty of the area. Still, some valleys such as the Greenstone lie outside the park with little protection from the plans to build a road from south of Kinloch up the wide river valley.

GETTING STARTED

The jumping-off place for all three tracks in Queenstown, a scenic village on the edge of Lake Wakatipu and across from the Remarkables range. Here arrangements can be made for transport to the trailheads, equipment secured and information obtained. It is also possible for solo travellers to meet up with other trampers through the message boards at the Youth Hostel Association or the Queenstown Motor Camp, one km from the centre of town. If Queenstown bustles in the winter with skiers, then it hops in the summer with trampers.

The park headquarters for Mt Aspiring National Park is in Wanaka with a ranger station in Glenorchy where most trampers record their intentions and obtain up-to-date information. The Government Tourist Bureau on Shotover St in Queenstown or the Department of Lands and Survey can also provide information. Queenstown is also the place for those interested in a guided trip on the Routeburn to relieve their shoulders of much of the load.

Getting to the tracks can sometimes be difficult and expensive affair. But once out there, you can easily jump from one to the other if the time and energy are there for more than one trek. To hit all three, hike up the Rees Valley, down the Dart, cross over the Routeburn and finish with the Greenstone-Caples before moving on to the Hollyford, Milford or a soft

mattress for a week. When coming off the Dart and moving on to the Rou-
burn, it is best to take the time to hike down to the Dart Bridge instead o.
fording the river at the trail's end. Most of the year the Dart is too swift
and deep to ford safely.

For those without transport from Queenstown, H&H Motors runs a bus
out to the Routeburn trailhead daily in January and every third day the rest
of the year. The only problem with the bus run is the small stampede at
the beginning of the trail as 10 to 40 trampers get started at the same time.
It is also possible for four or five hikers to split a cab fare to the track for
the same price as the bus or a few dollars more. Then there is always hitchhiking, but the pickings can be mighty slim on the road to Glenorchy and
even slimmer on the stretch after it.

H&H Motors will drop off trampers on the junction to the Rees Track
and from there it is six km to the trailhead or a 1½-hour hike. To get to just
the Greenstone-Caples Track, take the NZRRS bus from Te Anau to the
Divide and hike up the Routeburn to the start of the trail at Lake Howden.
The bus leaves Te Anau at 8.15 am, reaches the Divide around noon and
passes it on the way back between 4 and 5 pm. This is the same bus to catch
after finishing the Routeburn and heading south. Hitchhiking on the Milford
Highway is much easier than around Glenorchy. The trick is to time it with
those motorists visiting Milford Sound for a day, thumbing to the Sound in
the morning and to Te Anau in the afternoon.

For those with cars, access to the tracks can still be tricky. Somehow you
will have to make it back to your car at the Rees from the Dart or from
one end of the Routeburn to the other. It might be easier to leave vehicles
in Queenstown and use public transport.

All three tracks can be done in either direction. Most trampers, however,
will hike the Routeburn from east to west and the Greenstone Valley first
and then the Caples, saving the most scenic days for last. It is also easier to
climb up the gradually ascending Rees and return down the steep Dart
Valley.

The Routeburn can be walked in a single day if you are in shape and the
pack is light. But most first-time hikers will take three days, stopping at
Routeburn Falls and Lake Mackenzie for the night. An extra day should be
allowed as the impressive views from Harris Saddle will be missed if the
weather goes foul. If it doesn't, then the extra time can easily be spent
around Lake Mackenzie for a day's hike.

The Rees-Dart is usually done in four or five days. Nights are spent at
25-Mile Hut, Shelter Rock, Dart Hut, Daleys Hut and out on the fifth day;
or cut a day by hiking straight to Shelter Rock from the road on the first
day. The Greenstone-Caples takes three days with stops at the Mid-
Greenstone and Caples huts.

No special gear is needed for the tracks — just the usual good backpacking equipment of warm clothing, leak-proof rain gear and well broken-in
boots. The topographical maps, series one (1:63,360), to obtain are S122

for the Routeburn; S122 and S131 for the Greenstone-Caples; and S123, S144, S113 and S122 for the Rees-Dart. There are also recreation maps for Mt Aspiring National Park, Fiordland and Lake Wakatipu that cover the tracks in larger scale.

The tracks are rated mild for the Routeburn, a hard medium for the Rees-Dart and an easy medium for the Greenstone-Caples. Any tramper in good physical shape can undertake them without a guide. Caution should be used when crossing saddles during foul weather.

ROUTEBURN

The trip described goes from the trailhead north of Kinloch, over the Harris Saddle and eventually to the Milford Highway. One possibility for those who want to do a roundtrip on the Routeburn is to hike from Lake Mackenzie back to Routeburn Flats by way of Emily Pass. This is difficult, however, as the route is poorly marked, if marked at all in some places, and trampers have to be ready for untracked bush, scrub and stretches of deep snowgrass. Interested hikers should first consult the hut warden at Lake Mackenzie before attempting to climb.

Routeburn Shelter to Routeburn Falls

The track begins by crossing a swing bridge over the Routeburn and then climbs a benched trail on the north bank toward the Flats. Although the ascent seems mild, the track quickly comes to a gorge high above the river, reminding trampers of the alpine climb ahead. The track continues under a thick canopy of beech trees, crossing many small but swift-flowing streams. After a two-hour walk from the start, the trail breaks out into a gorge on the upper flats, crosses the Routeburn Stream again on another swing bridge and enters Routeburn Flats — a wide field of golden brown tussock. If the weather is clear, the Falls Hut will be visible, high above the flats.

The track winds through the Flats and comes to the junction to Routeburn Falls. The right-hand fork leads off to Flats Hut (20 bunks) 250 metres away, where the first night can be spent. The left-hand fork begins a sharp ascent to Falls Hut where most trampers will head the first day.

The climb is steep but quick and in an hour or so the track reaches the Falls Hut and the falls above the bushline. The view from the front porch of the hut is majestic, looking over the flats and surrounding Humboldt Mountains. There is no camping in the area of the huts or track, and wardens tend to be strict about enforcing this rule. If the hut is filled, trampers either sleep on the floor, tables or with each other; some even return to the much less used Flats Hut.

Accommodation: Flats Hut, 20 bunks; Falls Hut, 20 bunks.

Time: four hours

Routeburn Falls to Lake Mackenzie

The track continues behind the hut, passes the spectacular Routeburn Falls

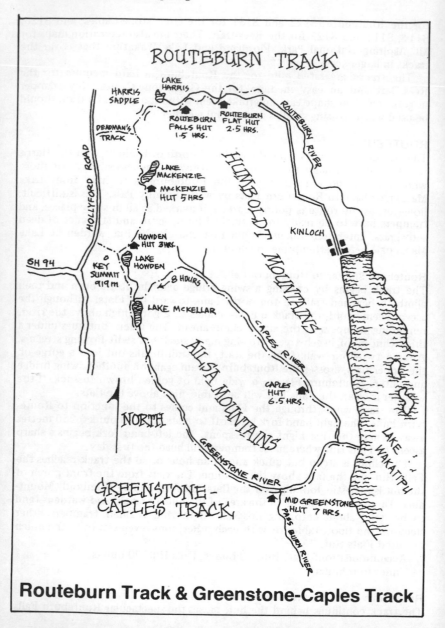

ROUTEBURN TRACK

LAKE HARRIS

HARRIS SADDLE

ROUTEBURN FALLS HUT 1.5 HRS.

ROUTEBURN FLAT HUT 2.5 HRS.

ROUTEBURN RIVER

DEADMAN'S TRACK

HOLLYFORD ROAD

HUMBOLDT MOUNTAINS

LAKE MACKENZIE

MACKENZIE HUT 5 HRS.

KINLOCH

SH 94

HOWDEN HUT 3 HRS.

LAKE HOWDEN

KEY SUMMIT 919 m

8 HOURS

LAKE McKELLAR

CAPLES RIVER

AILSA MOUNTAINS

CAPLES HUT 6.5 HRS.

LAKE WAKATIPU

NORTH

GREENSTONE RIVER

GREENSTONE-CAPLES TRACK

MID GREENSTONE HUT 7 HRS.

PASS BURN RIVER

Routeburn Track & Greenstone-Caples Track

and then begins climbing the final leg to Harris Saddle. At one point it passes through a flat tussock grassland where it is best to keep to the planks and avoid any encounters in with the bog. The track resumes its climb to Harris Saddle, passes an out-of-its hole square rock and ascends more steeply. Suddenly Lake Harris is there. The lakes takes away any other thoughts, especially on a clear day when the water reflects everything around.

At the 1277-metre level, there is a second jolt of unexpected views at the grassy meadows of Harris Saddle. The force of the wind and the mist can usually be felt on the saddle as the weather takes a switch on the exposed western side. The view also changes, from Lake Harris to the entire Hollyford Valley all the way to Martins Bay. For those with foul weather instead of beautiful views, there is an emergency shelter located on the saddle.

The track turns sharply south from the saddle and hangs on narrowly to the face of the ridge, high above the bushline for the best stretch of the trip. After 30 minutes, it arrives at the junction with Deadman's Track, an extremely steep, five-hour route to the floor of the Hollyford Valley. Further down the track, 45 minutes from Deadman's junction, is a huge rock bivouac that can be used as an emergency shelter or a place to stay for those who want to avoid people or the hut fee at Lake Mackenzie. The rock is a few metres off to the right of the track and deep enough underneath for comfortable lodging and an intimate night with the surrounding alpine countryside.

Two hours from the saddle, the track ascends and works around a spur, exposing Lake Mackenzie, a jewel set in a small green mountain valley. The track begins a zig-zag pattern down to the lake, dropping sharply the final 300 metres to the valley floor. Just before the treeline, a rock with a plaque dedicated to a pair of lost trampers reminds those passing by of ever present alpine danger.

Finally the track reaches the bottom, skirts through lush bush again and around the southern end of the lake before arriving at one of the most deluxe huts any park can boast of in New Zealand.

Accommodation: rock bivouac, sleeps four; Lake Mackenzie Hut, 40 bunks.

Time: five hours.

Lake Mackenzie to Milford Rd

The track begins in front of the hut, goes past the private hut and through a tussock meadow before climbing for an hour. Gradually it makes up for the lost height from the descent to Lake Mackenzie and breaks out of the bush briefly with good views of the Hollyford and the Darran Mountains across the valley. The track moves close to the mountainside and after two hours arrives at the thundering Earland Falls, an ideal spot for an extended break. The spray will fog up camera lenses and quickly cool any overheated tramper on a sunny day. If it is raining, the falls will be twice as powerful. There is a swing bridge nearby to cross a flooded stream.

The track improves in the next hour and suddenly opens up to Lake Howden, a major junction of the area. The lake can be spectacular on a still day with brilliant reflections of the surrounding mountains on its surface. From here other tracks go north to the Hollyford Rd or south to the Greenstone Track; to the west is the remainder of the Routeburn and Key Summit.

The track swings by the flanks of Key Summit and a side trip can be made through the bush to the open tops of the peak. The view from here includes the Hollyford, Greenstone and Eglinton valleys, and overwhelms most who take the time to scale the peak. From Key Summit, the track quickly drops to the bush level where thick rainforest resumes. Finally the trail arrives at the Milford Rd and the road shelter for those waiting for a bus or hitching a ride.

Accommodation: Lake Howden Hut, 15 bunks; roadside shelter, no bunks.

Time: four hours.

REES-DART TRACK
This trip is described up the Rees River and down the Dart, the easiest way of hiking the route. For those who choose to go up the Dart and down the Rees, additional time should be allowed, especially from Dart Hut to Shelter Rock via Rees Saddle.

McDougalls Creek to Shelter Rock
A four-wheel-drive road leads up the Rees Valley to 25-Mile Hut, but most vehicles have problems reaching that point. Trampers generally begin the trail at McDougalls Creek while those without private transport might have to hike in from the road junction, an additional six km or another hour and half. Either way, many make 25-Mile Hut their first stop and take five days to hike the track, instead of pushing to Shelter Rock. To use 25-Mile Hut, permission should be obtained from the Otago Tramping Club (PO Box 1120, Dunedin).

The track from McDougalls Creek is easy to follow as it passes Invincible and Muddy Creeks, sites of intense mining activity back in the 19th century. Beyond Muddy Creek, there is a choice: the old track follows the river bank and is usually preferred in good weather; the new route off to the right works its way higher in the hills, avoiding rising streams and creeks during heavy rainfalls.

After Bridges Creek, the track turns into wide-flowing tussock grasslands with impressive views of glaciers clinging between the peaks of the Forbes Mountains. Along the way it passes two private huts between Bridges and Arthur's Creek and then slowly reveals the summit of Mt Earnslaw, a towering peak at 2819 metres.

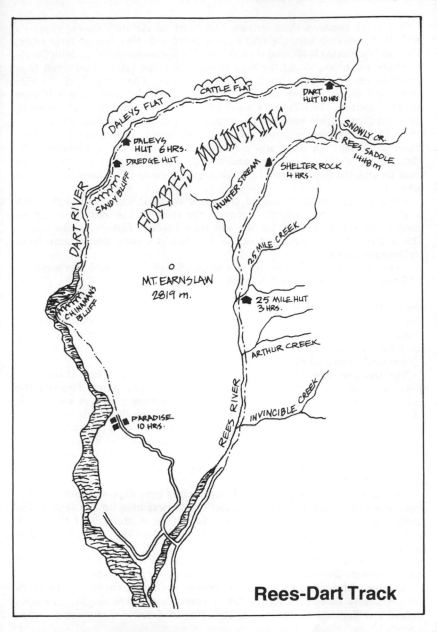

Rees-Dart Track

The track passes a third private hut north of Arthur's Creek, crosses a bluff then descends into the flats leading to 25-Mile Hut, just an hour away. The hut (six bunks) is located on a terrace 70 metres south of 25-Mile Creek.

Those intent on doing the trail in four days can take a break and then continue on to Shelter Rock, four hours away. The track fords 25-Mile Creek and works its way off the terrace towards the river. Above Hunter Stream junction, the Rees is crossed by a footbridge and the trail moves to the west (true right) bank and completely abandons the four-wheel-drive track. Here the flats disappear and the beech forest closes in until the track clears the bush. An hour and a half from 25-Mile Hut, it descends into Clarke Slip, a hidden meadow and pleasant camping spot for those who want to end the first day in a tent. More grassy campsites follow in the next hour's tramping.

From the end of the grassland, the track works its way up through beech forest to open scrubland, then crosses the river to the east bank and to Shelter Rock Hut, named for the old rock bivouac further up the valley. The hut is new, sleeps ten but can be reached in a good day's tramp from McDougalls Creek.

Accommodation: 25-Mile Hut, six bunks; Shelter Rock Hut, ten bunks.

Time: seven hours to Shelter Rock.

Shelter Rock to Dart Hut

The walk from Shelter Rock over the saddle to Dart Hut should not be taken lightly. Trampers should have reasonably good weather and an early start for the full day ahead of them. The walk takes most hikers eight to 10 hours with normal pack loads.

The track resumes in scrub and then moves into flats where it fords the Rees, a small creek now, and continues up the east bank. Towards the saddle, the track passes through an incredible tussock grassland with a view of Earnslaw in the south and, in early summer, alpine flowers at every turn. For those with extra days, this is one place to camp on a pleasant evening. The track passes through and begins its steep climb to the Rees Saddle, the lowest point on the ridge at 1450 metres. In the final 100 metres, there is steep snowgrass. A cave on the Rees side of the saddle can be used for shelter during foul weather.

The alpine environment is worth some extra time exploring but the view from the saddle can be somewhat limited. A scramble up the spur to the south-east takes two hours and offers an extensive outlook of the valley and surrounding mountains. The track moves out of the saddle and begins to make its way down towards the gorge created by Snowy Creek. The route is well marked with orange poles, but has the most potential danger of any section of the track with its steep and slippery grass slopes that become even more slippery after rain. Just before the gorge closes in, the track crosses Snowy Creek on a footbridge and then begins climbing for 30 metres before levelling out to the north. It begins to descend steeply again when the junction of Snowy Creek and the Dart come into view before finally crossing Snowy a second time on another footbridge and arriving at the hut.

Accommodation: Dart Hut, twenty bunks.

Time: Eight to 10 hours.

Dart Hut to Daleys Hut

The track descends towards Cattle Flat from Dart Hut and runs through an old creek bed reaching the junction of the trail to Whitbourn Flat. Caution should be exercised in the dry stream bed as the track can easily be lost. The right-hand fork leads to a bridge across the Dart at the Whitbourn junction

thick forest is broken by Quinns Flat which the track passes through. It then begins a climb over a low saddle and into Daleys Flat, entering in the eastern corner away from the river. It moves closer to the river and finally arrives at the park hut at the south end of the flat.

Accommodation: Daleys Hut, 20 bunks

Time: six hours

Daleys Hut to Paradise

The track is easy to follow from Daleys Flat as it stays close to the river and then breaks out onto Dredge Flat, site of the Dredge Hut, built in 1900 during an unsuccessful attempt to mine gold. All materials, including a complete sawmill plant with a boiler, were hauled up in wagons from Glenorchy in what had to be a monumental task.

The track climbs steeply towards Sandy Bluff and then is benched into the bluff before descending for 100 metres to Sandy Flat. From here the forest is less overpowering as numerous grass clearings break it up and great bluffs, carved by the river, dominate the scene. Just beyond Sandy Bluff, the Sisters — bush-covered rocks — appear in the middle of the channel, forcing the water to go elsewhere. From the flats there are also good views of the Cosmos and Bride peaks.

After Sisters Rocks, the track proceeds to Bedford Stream, crossing it by a footbridge, and then winds through forest and flats to a terrace that leads to Survey Creek and Survey Flats. It leaves the flat and terrace and briefly becomes an old bridle track at a small beach before arriving at Chinaman's Bluff. The track skirts around the bluff and connects with a four-wheel-drive track. This leads through Chinaman's Flat and then Dan's Paddock, a 1½-km clearing. The track crosses Dundas Creek and breaks out of the bush into grazing land at Mill Flat, remaining in this landscape until Paradise. The walk from Daleys Hut to Paradise is 10 hours long, less if a ride is caught from the end of the road to the small village.

Time: 10 hours.

GREENSTONE-CAPLES TRACK

Although this track can be done in either direction, the following description goes down the Greenstone and then back up the Caples, saving the most scenic areas for last.

Lake Howden to Mid-Greenstone Hut

The track begins on the south side of Lake Howden Hut and is well marked as it leads around the west side of the lake, over the Greenstone Saddle and around the west side of Lake McKellar, passing the junction to Caples Valley. Three hours from the beginning, the track arrives at a bridge just below Lake McKellar and crosses over to the east bank of the river and into Greenstone Flats. Here the track is again well marked and developed as it runs down the flats, arriving across the river from the private Rat's Nest Hut, an hour and half from the bridge.

Following the flats, the track passes a deep chasm that thunders with the river below. The view from here of the surrounding area is spectacular. An hour from Rat's Nest, the track leaves the river side and swings to the east to avoid swamps and bog areas. It crosses Steele Creek and arrives at the Mid-Greenstone Hut, one km below the stream on a terrace next to the edge of the bush.

Accommodation: Mid-Greenstone Hut, 12 bunks.

Time: seven hours.

Mid-Greenstone Hut to Caples Hut

The track resumes on the terrace along the bush edge, following the river for almost an hour before climbing into the bush at the beginning of the flats across the Pass Burn junction. The track continues to sidle the bush above the flats; for an alternative route you can tramp through the flats, staying close to the river. Eventually the track ascends high above the Greenstone Gorge where the valley swings left, and within an hour and a half from Pass Burn descends to the western end of Big Slip, also known as Slip Flat. It follows the river closely and passes a small two-bunk hut in the flats, built and administered by NZFS. Big Slip hut is the place to spend the night for those who want to complete the trip in two days instead of the usual three, but this is only possible if you are fit and prepared. The second day from the hut up the Caples and back to Lake Howden is an extra-long hike of 10-12 hours.

From Big Slip, the track follows the gorge for a short distance and comes to the junction to Elfin Bay. The right-hand fork crosses a bridge and continues on to the bay that once was the main access to the Greenstone Valley. The other fork is the route that was built in 1977 through the rest of the gorge to a swing bridge that spans the Greenstone just before the junction with the Caples River. Crossing the bridge, this track continues to the mouth of the Greenstone. The left-hand fork leads away from the Greenstone and up the Caples Valley on the western bank. In two hours, it passes an airstrip and the old Birchdale Homestead on a high terrace. The track climbs above the homestead and to the Caples Hut, which is located up the left side of the terrace after a small gorge.

Accommodation: Big Slip Hut, two bunks; Caples Hut, 12 bunks.

Time: 6½ hours.

Caples Hut to Upper Greenstone

The track leaves Caples Hut and continues on the west bank of the river. It arrives at a large flat at the western end of the valley floor then a small one at the valley tip 20 minutes later. The track then ascends 150 metres from the valley floor, passing the junction between the Caples and Fraser Creeks and reaching a boggy meadow where one could camp if forced by necessity.

The track continues to climb and is marked in most of the open sections by metal standards. It crosses over a dry stream bed, fords the Caples — now a mountain creek — to the north and climbs 200 metres on true right of the river. After passing beneath a knob to the south, the track crosses the Caples for the last time and begins its final ascent to the saddle.

The saddle is bush-free and usually swampy, but an easy passage to Lake McKellar. The track moves through it, quickly descends 100 metres and turns north for a few hundred metres more. It drops again with a series of switchbacks north and eventually breaks out of the bush at the head of Lake McKellar where it runs into the Greenstone Track to complete the circular trip. Further up the track, another 40-60 minutes, is the Lake Howden Hut.

Accommodation: Lake Howden Hut, 15 bunks.

Time: eight hours.

South Island — Fiordland

Milford Track
Hollyford Track
Lake Hauroko-Supper Cove-West Arm

The defence seems impenetrable. Mountain ranges with granite peaks flank one side; the Tasman Sea guards the other. The interior is slashed by steep-sided fiords while the entire area is doused by rain and hidden in misty shroud. In Fiordland, nature is makings its final stance against technology and the changing world people so often bring with them. Among the lakes, mountains and forests, humans come as visitors but rarely as permanent residents.

That is the magic of Fiordland, called New Zealand's Final Frontier by many. Although a few areas are heavily used and visited, all are a trip back into time and a journey away from the sights, sounds and smells of modern society. If the area seems hard to get to or expensive to travel into, it is only a small price to pay for keeping preserved the natural wonders of New Zealand's most dramatic wilderness.

Fiordland is the largest national park in New Zealand and possibly the largest in the Southern Hemisphere at 1.2 million hectares. It stretches from Martins Bay in the north to Preservation Inlet in the South. In between lie 14 of some of the most beautiful fiords to be found, and certainly the best collection of waterfalls. The rugged terrain, combined with the thick bush and the abundance of water are the elements that kept people and progress out yesterday and today are the major appeal of the area to trampers and tourists from around the world.

Fiordland was a complex recipe, created by several geological processes. The first was sediment gradually building on the sea bottom to form the oldest rocks more than 300 million years ago. A period of mountain folding followed, together with metamorphism of the sediments and intrusion of granites, before the area was covered again by the sea for another 40 million years. But the most important era to Fiordland's majestic shaping were the periods of glaciation in the last million years and as recently as 15,000 years ago. The glaciers sharpened the peaks, gouged the fiords and lakes and carved the rounded valleys. The evidence of the ice flows can be found almost everywhere from the moraine terraces behind Te Anau township, all along Eglinton's rounded valley to the pointed peaks of the Milford Sound.

One result of the geological forces is Fiordland's distinct trademark of lakes. Te Anau is the largest lake in the South Island and second largest in the country. It is 66 km long, with a shoreline of 500 km and an area of 342 sq km, and is the access point for most of Fiordland's scenic attractions. Lake Hauroko, the main access to Dusky Sound and Supper Cove, is the deepest lake in New Zealand with a depth of 463 metres. And parts of Lake McKerrow are claimed by many to offer the best trout fishing in the South Island.

Another result of Fiordland's glacial upbringing is its trademark of waterfalls. The sheerness of the mountain walls and fiords have created ideal conditions for waterfalls, and there seems to be one at every bend of every track, cascading, tumbling, roaring or simply dribbling down a green mossy bluff. The most famous is the Sutherland Falls on the Milford Track with its three magnificent leaps and a total drop of 580 metres, making it the third highest in the world. By the end of any trip backpackers become connoisseurs of waterfalls, viewing their shapes, drops and force with an artist's eye. Some even secretly pray for rain that will produce twice as many, twice as powerful along the tracks.

Fiordland has come to symbolize waterfalls, lakes, fiords — and rain, buckets of the stuff. Weather is predominantly wet year-round with storms and winds moving west from the Tasman Sea and dumping up to 7600 mm of rain on the coast and western portion of the park. Early morning mist and thick layers of fog are quite common in the southern region. Behind the mountains and the lake, Te Anau township receives 1000 mm of rain a year.

The large amounts of moisture mean lush vegetation, as well as waterfalls. On the eastern side, forests of red, silver and mountain beech fill the valleys and cling to the sides of steep faces. In the northern and western coastal sections impressive podocarps forest of matai, rimu, northern rata and totara can be found. Much of the forest can be seen growing on the surface of hard rock, covered by only a thin layer of rich humus and moss, a natural retainer for the large amounts of rain. It is this peaty carpet that allows thick ground flora to thrive under towering canopies and sets western Fiordland bush apart from the rest of the country.

The birdlife is also distinctive. Not only is it abundant with a wide variety of native species, but it also contains two types of flightless birds rarely found in New Zealand. The Takahe, not seen for 50 years and feared to be extinct, was rediscovered in 1948 on the western shore of Lake Te Anau, creating a major stir throughout the ornithological world. A large, heavily-built bird, the takahe stands 45 cm high and is brightly coloured with scarlet feet and bill, and feathers that range from blue to olive-green. Research has placed the takahe population at less than 150 birds, most of which live in the Murchison Mountains west of Lake Te Anau.

Even more rare, however, is the kakapo, a nocturnal ground parrot found in a few valleys and watersheds of the Milford and Sutherland Sounds. The male, a large green bird which can glide but not fly, has a mating habit of booming from steep ridges in search of a mate. Unfortunately no female has been sighted recently in Fiordland where 12 heartsick males boom forlornly.

Both species were almost reduced to extinction by the stoat and ferret, small ground animals introduced in the area to control the rampaging (and also introduced) rabbit populations. Both have devastating effects on all birdlife, but especially gorund dwelling birds which never developed a natural defence against such predators. Still some flightless birds surviving in strong numbers, most notably the weka and the kiwi which can be found through much of the national park. The national bird is often sighted by persistent kiwi watchers in areas west of Lakes Te Anau and Manapouri and occasionally along the Milford Track close to the Sound. Bush birds most likely to be spotted are the kaka and kea (forest and alpine parrots), wood pigeons, fantails, bush robins, tuis, bellbirds, cuckoos, and parakeets.

Trampers will also encounter something else buzzing through the air — the sandfly. Fiordland has more than its share of them. There is an exceptionally high proportion around Martins Bay, most of the Hollyford Track and several points along the Milford Track, including the end which has been appropriately named Sandfly Point. In alpine regions or in wind, rain, direct sun or cold spells, the sandfly's numbers are reduced significantly, but rarely does it disappear completely. There are also mosquitoes in a few areas. But the insect that captures the fancy of hikers is the glow-worm. Their bluish light is most spectacular in the Te Ana-au Caves where they line the walls by the thousands. They can easily be spotted on most tracks glowing at dusk or at night beneath the ferns and heavy ground bush that is sharply cut across by the trail.

Other wildlife in the park includes wapiti (elk) and red deer, both of which are widely hunted, and chamois. Also hunted are pigs, goats and opossums, which have caused widespread damage by their overwhelming numbers. Fiordland is well known for rainbow and brown trout fishing in many of its hundreds of clear, cold, fast-running streams. There is also excellent coastal fishing, especially at Martins Bay and Supper Cove.

Improved road access and tourist facilities over the years have opened up much of the park that in the past was virtually forbidden to the visitor. There are boat launches on many of the lakes and fiords, bus trips to the Milford Sound and a wide range of airplane flights that enable you to see much of the area in a short amount of time. Still, the most intimate and personally rewarding way of experiencing the wonder of Fiordland is the oldest — on foot on almost 500 km of tracks and routes in the park. The tracks, most well maintained combined with more than 60 huts scattered along them, allow the tramper the greatest access to the area.

Unquestionably the most famous in New Zealand and around the world is the Milford Track, labelled by many as the 'finest walk in the world'. The Milford is almost a religious crusade to most Kiwis for if they never do another walk, they must hike this 54-km trail. Right from the beginning the Milford has been a highly regulated and commercial venture which deters many trampers from doing it. But by enduring the high costs, mileposts, telephone wires and the abundance of huts, shelters and wooden walkways, you are rewarded with some of the most spectacular scenery in New Zealand.

There are, however, other tracks in Fiordland outside of the Milford. The Hollyford stretches from the end of the Lower Hollyford Rd out to isolated Martins Bay and is steeped in history, lore and outstanding fishing holes. At the southern tip is the eight-day trek from Lake Hauroko to Supper Cove of Dusky Sound back to the West Arm of Lake Manapouri. Both tracks are considerably more difficult than the Milford, both take special arrangements to get in and out, but both offer something the Milford never can — solitude in a wilderness area not over-run by signposts, guided parties or park workers with gas-powered weed cutters.

HISTORY

In comparison with other regions of the country, little is known of the pre-European history of the Maoris in Fiordland. There is evidence of a permanent settlement at Martins Bay and possibly summer villages at Te Anau and Preservation Inlet, used for seasonal hunting expeditions into the area.

The most significant find, however, occurred in 1967 when G H Evans discovered the remains of a Maori sitting burial in a small, dry cave on Mary Island in Lake Hauroko. It was the best preserved burial ever recovered and possibly one of the oldest. The body was that of a woman, presumably a high-ranking one, and dated back to the mid-1600s. During Cook's second voyage, he made contact with three parties of friendly natives, one bold enough to come aboard the ship and fire a musket three times. But Cook never sighted any large or permanent settlements, and neither did any explorer who followed him. Obviously Fiordland was an important hunting ground and a source of greenstone for the Maoris, but not a place to linger.

Cook first arrived in the *Endeavour* in 1770 and worked his way up the west coast, attempting to land at several of the sounds. He was unsuccessful as dusk arrived too soon in one, while at another he was doubtful about the direction of the wind. When the great sea captain departed he left names on a map, but never a mark in the soil. Cook returned three years later when he brought *Resolution* into Dusky Sound to recuperate after a three-month voyage at sea. Recorded in his log in 1773 was the crew's seal hunt, the first in New Zealand, and probably the first written description of sand-flies — 'most mischievous animals . . . that cause a swelling not possible to refrain from scratching'.

Cook's midshipman, George Vancouver, returned to Fiordland in 1791, taking his ship up Dusky Sound as his former captain had. The following year a sealing gang of 12 men were left in the Sound for a few months where they reaped a harvest of 4500 skins, constructed one of the first buildings in New Zealand and nearly completed a ship with the emergency iron work left behind. They were taken away by the mother ship, but more sealers returned and by 1795 there were about 250 people in Dusky Sound. By the turn of the century there was a regular sealing trade in the sounds. It took but a few more years to slaughter most of the seals in the area, putting a quick finish to the industry.

Whaling moved in briefly in 1829 when the first station of any size in the South Island was built at Perservation Inlet. In six seasons it produced 500 tonnes of oil. By 1838, however, the station was abandoned and the industry had only a meagre foothold in Fiordland after that. The two industries did promote exploration of the coast as Welsh sealing captain John Grono became the first to sail into the Milford Sound in 1823, naming it after his hometown of Milford Haven.

Fiordland continued to be explored from the sea until runholder C J Nairn reached Lake Te Anau in 1852 from the Waiau Valley. Nine years later two more cattle drivers, David McKellar and George Gunn, climbed to the top of Key Summit and became the first to view the Hollyford Valley. It was Patrick Caples, however, who was the first to descend into the Hollyford from the Routeburn Pass in 1863. Caples reached Martins Bay but didn't stick around too long as smoke from some Maori fires scared him back into the bush.

A few months later Captain Alabaster made his way from Martins Bay to Lake Howden and was followed by James Hector who worked up the Hollyford and eventually back to Queenstown to a hero's welcome from the miners. Each man thought he was the first to make the journey as news and communications travelled along a slower path then.

Miners continued to move deeper into Fiordland in search of the one golden stream that would take care of them for life. In 1868, the Otago Provincial Government added its stimulus to the area's growth when it decided to start a settlement at Martins Bay. The town was surveyed on the north-east corner of Lake McKerrow, named Jamestown, and many of its lots sold. But a black cloud settled over the town, and right from the beginning Jamestown had to struggle to exist in the desolate region. The road down the Hollyford was never built as two attempts proved hopeless. Ships, meanwhile, had an extremely hard time navigating the river's entrance and many simply gave up during rough seas and sailed on without dropping off their vital supplies.

A   Lake Harris on the Routeburn Track
B   The Southern Alps near Mt Aspiring National Park

A
B

The settlers that finally moved into the area found life hard and most of the time lonely. By 1870 there were eight houses in Jamestown, but nine years later the settlement was completely deserted with only a handful of people continuing to live in Martins Bay. The only other permanent residents in Fiordland at the time were two hermits who settled in the sounds during the 1870s. One was William Docherty, who after earning his prospecting licence, settled in Dusky Sound in 1877 and stayed until the late 1890s. The other was Donald Sutherland, a colourful character who sailed 100 km from Thompson Sound into Milford Sound in 1877 and became known as the 'Hermit of Milford'.

In 1880, Sutherland and John Mackay struggled up the Arthur valley from Milford in search of precious minerals. Instead they found a fine waterfall which Mackay left his name on after winning a coin toss. After several more days of labouring through the thick bush, they sighted a magnificent three-leap waterfall and of course it was only fair that Sutherland immediately stuck his name on this one. The pair then stumbled up to the Mackinnon Pass, viewed the Clinton River and returned to the sound.

Gradually word of Sutherland's Falls leaked back to towns and cities and the number of adventurers determined to see the natural wonder increased, as did the pressure for a track or road to the Milford area. Efforts to find a pass from Lake Te Anau to the sound began in 1888 when Quintin Mackinnon and Ernest Mitchell, with the financial support and blessing of the government, set out to cut a route along the Clinton River. Moving up through the Arthur Valley at the same time was C W Adams, chief surveyor of Otago, and his party of 11. In October of 1888, Mackinnon and Mitchell quit track cutting and scrambled over the pass, spent an icy night above the bushline and then made their way past the present site of the Quintin Huts to meet Adams urged quick development of it as a tourist track. A rough trail was finished, a few flimsy huts thrown up and by 1890 tourists, including the first woman, were using the route with Mackinnon as a guide. The government continued to seek improvements of the track and huts and in 1903 the Government Tourist Department took over all facilities on the track, including the ferry running on Lake Te Anau to the trailhead.

While the Milford Sound was attracting people, Martins Bay was driving them away. By the turn of the century, the McKenzie brothers, Malcolm and Hugh, were the sole inhabitants of the area, using a rough track in the Hollyford Valley to drive their cattle to the stockyards. In 1926, the

A A Milford Sound at the end of the Milford Track
B C B On the Hollyford Track — Lake McKerrow reflecting Mt Tutoko
     C The spectacular Sutherland Falls on the Milford Track

brothers sold out to Davy Gunn, a Scotsman from Invercargill.

Gunn became a legend in his own time. He improved the track in the valley, constructed huts along the way and gradually went from runholding cattle to guiding tourists down the Hollyford River. Gunn's greatest achievement, however, was the emergency trip he undertook to reach help for victims of an aircraft crash in Big Bay in 1936. Gunn tramped from Big Bay to Lake McKerrow, rowed up the lake and then rode his horse more than 40 km to a construction camp where he telephoned for another plane. The trip would take an experienced hiker three days; Gunn did it in 21 hours. He continued his single-handed promotion of the valley until 1955 when he drowned in the Hollyford River after his horse slipped on the track. Today his son, Murray Gunn, maintains a motor camp and a museum dedicated to his father and the settlers of Martins Bay.

The Milford Track changed significantly in 1940 when trampers could walk through the Homer Tunnel. Up to that point most hikers had to turn around at the sound and backtrack along the trail. In 1954 the tunnel, which began as a relief workers project in the 1930s, was finally opened up to motor traffic. Two years before that Fiordland National Park was created, preserving a million hectares and protecting the route to the Milford Sound.

Up to 1965, the track and hut facilities were controlled by the Tourist Hotel Corporation and trampers had to take park of the guided trip to walk the trail. A protest and demonstration in front of the THC Hotel in the sound brought about the changes and creation of huts for 'freedom walkers'. Today both guided trampers and freedom walkers share the track but use different huts along the way.

Fiordland was finally rounded out to its present 1.2 million hectares in 1960 when the Hollyford Valley and Martins Bay were included in the national park.

GETTING STARTED

Te Anau, a small town on the eastern shore of Lake Te Anau, is the home of the Fiordland National Park Headquarters, the jumping off spot for the Milford Track and the centre for most of the boat launches and commercial trips into the region. Here you can generally find anything or hire any kind of service you need to complete your plans in Fiordland.

The park headquarters located on the Te Anau Terrace beside the lake, is open daily, and has information or handouts for any part or track in the park. This is also the place to make reservations to walk the Milford Track or leave your intentions before departing on a trek of any nature. There is also an unmanned ranger station in Clifden, open 24 hours a day where most trampers attempting the Lake Hauroko-Supper Cove-West Arm trip check in and leave their plans.

Making all the necessary arrangements for the Milford can often be harder than walking the 54-km track. The first step is to get a reservation. If you have a large party and want to walk during late December or January, book ahead — way ahead, if possible. Reservations often come six months in advance and with only 24 spots open for each day on the track, it doesn't take long for them to fill up. If you are travelling alone or in a pair and can wait a few days, getting on the Milford is considerably easier. Often there are cancellations that allow you to depart for the trail almost immediately. By mid-February the reservations begin to slow as the summer rush is over and by March the limit of 24 freedom walkers is often not reached.

Once the reservation is secured, you pay the hut fee to the park head-quarters. This covers the fee for three nights in the huts and the launch from Sandfly Point to Milford. The next step is to jog down the street to Fiord-land Travel right along the lake and purchase a launch ticket to take you from Te Anau Downs across the lake to the trailhead. If you are without your own transport, also purchase a bus ticket from them to Te Anau Downs. The bus leaves Fiordland Travel from November through mid-April, to meet with the launch that departs from Te Anau Downs.

One last stop you might make is the NZRS station in town for transport from Milford back to Te Anau or Queenstown. Buses leave Milford twice daily, morning and afternoon. The afternoon run is important to independent walkers for it allows them to come off the track and catch a ride back, avoiding a costly night staying at Milford. Accommodation at the Sound includes a THC lodge, a private lodge run by THC and a campground a few km out the road, renowned for its sandfly population. The NZRS station is also the place to forward extra gear on to your next stop.

The Milford is tightly regulated, a bitter point with many trampers who don't like every step pre-planned for them. You must walk the track in one direction from Glade House to the sound during the summer season. You must stay at Clinton Forks the first night, despite it being only a two-hour walk from the trailhead, and you must complete the trip in the allowed three nights, four days. The time limit is perhaps the most discouraging aspect of the Milford. After all the planning and expense to walk the track, if the weather goes sour you still push on and cross the alpine section. Unlike the Routeburn or any other track in New Zealand, you can't wait out a day or two for good weather or clear views.

Freedom walkers and guided hikers are kept apart by using separate huts and launch trips. Credit has to be given to the system for rarely will a freedom walker see a guided party. With careful segregation and the one-way travel, the Milford looks much less crowded than you might expect with 7000 hikers crossing it every year. My personal recommendation is to hike it in March when the crowds are gone and the weather, many believe, is usually drier.

Although reservations are certainly not needed, the Hollyford and Lake Hauroko-Supper Cove-West Arm Tracks still take a bit of planning to tackle. Hollyford is a four or five-day tramp out to Martins Bay, with several options on how to return. You can backtrack the 70 km to the Hollyford Rd or turn the trip into a 10-day, circular trek by hiking around the Big

Bay, over to the Pyke River, down the river and Lake Alabaster and eventually back to the original track to the road's end. The easiest way of returning, however, is to catch a flight from Martins Bay back to the airstrip below Gunn's Camp. Hollyford Tourist and Travel Co, which runs guided trips up the valley, will often fly freedom walkers either out to the bay or back depending on when they are running an empty plane out to pick up clients. The flight is fairly expensive but is a pleasant way to end a tramp out in the valley.

The same company also runs jet-boat trips on Lake McKerrow for their clients and again will take trampers up the lake, by-passing the hardest section of the track and saving a day's struggle along the Demon Trail. The company's main office is in Invercargill; the address is PO Box 216.

Once out in Martins Bay, two thirds are needed — spare time and good insect dope. The isolated bay is a great spot to spend an extra day as it offers superb coastal and trout fishing, as well as a view of one of the most interesting seal colonies in New Zealand. The park hut is new, situated in a beautiful spot and even equipped with hooks and lines. Sandflies and mosquitoes are both present and make quick introductions to all trampers passing through.

The trailhead begins at the end of the Lower Hollyford Rd, 16 km from the junction with the Milford Highway. Those without transport can take a bus to the junction and hitch a ride, given enough time, to Gunn's Camp. From the motor camp to the trailhead, a distance of eight km, the thumbing is difficult and many trampers end up hiking an extra two hours to reach the track. When returning from the track, the story is the same: poor hitching from the trailhead. For this reason many spend a night at Gunn's Camp where Murray rents out basic bunk-and-table cabins and tent space. He also carries a good selection of backpackers' food and supplies in his store, everything from single candles to single eggs. Trampers coming off the Routeburn can restock here before moving on to the Hollyford. If travelling through, you should also take in Murray's museum, devoted to his father and the Martins Bay settlers. The artifacts hanging on the wall combined with a few late night stories from Murray will fill your head with the lore and legends of those who preceded you down the Hollyford.

Although a ranger resides in Clifden, Tautapere is the starting point for most hikers attempting the Lake Hauroko-Supper Cove-West Arm Track. The trail can be begun either from Lake Hauroko or Lake Manapouri, but many prefer ending at Lake Manapouri and spending their first night off the track at Te Anau rather than Tuatapere. H&H Motors runs a bus from Invercargill to Tuatapere Monday through Friday leaving late afternoon. At Tuatapere, make arrangements with Val McKay who takes trampers to the lake and ferries them over to the trailhead.

Before departing on the track, you should also have arrangements secured for your pick-up at the West Arm of Lake Manapouri. Fiordland Travel (PO Box 1, Te Anau) runs regular morning and afternoon cruises to the West Arm and will pick up trampers coming off the track. They also provide a bus service between Manapouri and Te Anau that connects with all launch trips.

Because of the large amounts of rain on any of the three tracks, rain gear — jacket and pants — is essential, as is having everything in your pack stored in plastic bags, especially your sleeping bag. Bring insect dope. Those planning to spend a few days at Martins Bay might even consider bringing mosquito netting. Since the Lake Hauroko-Supper Cove-West Arm trip is at least eight days long, double check your food supply and make sure a good portion of it is freeze-dried meal packets. They cost more, but the savings in weight can be considerable for the total trip.

The Fiordland recreation map, FNP 273, covers all three tracks, but for more detail of the areas obtain the series one topographical maps S105 and S113 for the Hollyford, S121 and S122 for the Milford, and S148 and S157 for the Lake Hauroko-Supper Cove-West Arm.

MILFORD TRACK
Most trampers take the launch across Lake Te Anau, a pleasant trip that is a good introduction to the area. One alternative to the lake cruise is to hike over the Dore Pass to reach the trailhead from the Eglinton Valley. The route is a hard one, however, and should be undertaken only by experienced trampers with good mountaineering skills.

Lake Wharf to Clinton Forks
The track from the wharf is a wide tractor path which was once used by packhorses to carry in supplies to the various huts. After about 15 minutes, it passes Glade House, the official start of the Milford Track, and then crosses the Clinton River on a large swing bridge. From here the track continues as a wide gentle path where no stone or blade of grass appears out of place.

At one point the track passes an impressive view of the summits next to Dore Pass before re-entering the thick bush along the river. This section of the Clinton River to a few km past the Forks Hut is a fisherman's dream and quite often trout or eels can be seen knifing through deep, clear pools.

The track passes through Black Forest, an area of dark tree trunks and a mediaeval appearance, and then comes to the junction with Clinton Forks Hut. This is where independent walkers must spend their first night; the guided parties spend the night at Glade House.

Accommodation: Clinton Forks Hut, 24 bunks.

Time: two hours.

Clinton Forks to Mintaro Hut
The track leaves Clinton Forks and heads for Six-Mile Hut where the valley becomes noticeably narrower with granite walls boxing in both sides of the river. In many places a layer of moss covers the valley walls with mountain

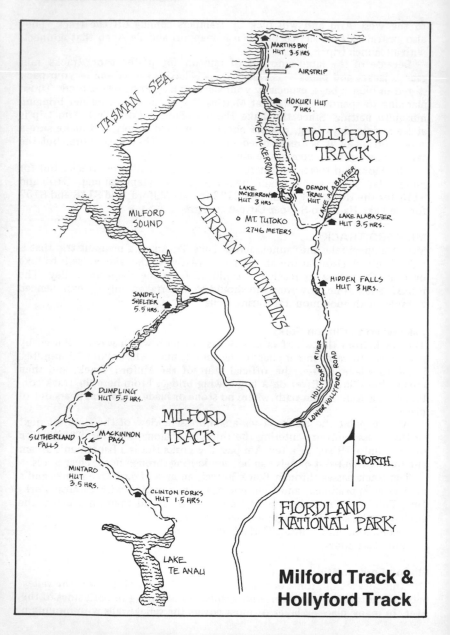

MARTINS BAY
HUT
3.5 HRS.

AIRSTRIP

TASMAN SEA

HOKURI HUT
7 HRS.

LAKE McKERROW

HOLLYFORD
TRACK

LAKE McKERRON
HUT 3 HRS.

DEMON
TRAIL
HUT

LAKE ALABASTER

o MT. TUTOKO
2746 METERS

LAKE ALABASTER
HUT 3.5 HRS.

MILFORD
SOUND

DARRAN MOUNTAINS

HIDDEN FALLS
HUT 3 HRS.

SANDFLY
SHELTER
5.5 HRS.

HOLLYFORD RIVER

HOLLYFORD ROAD

DUMPLING
HUT 5.5 HRS.

MILFORD
TRACK

LOWER HOLLYFORD ROAD

SUTHERLAND
FALLS

MACKINNON PASS

NORTH

MINTARO
HUT
3.5 HRS.

CLINTON FORKS
HUT 1.5 HRS.

FIORDLAND
NATIONAL PARK

LAKE
TE ANAU

**Milford Track &
Hollyford Track**

streams dribbling straight to the valley floor like an artistic fountain in a downtown plaza. The track passes Six-Mile Hut, a lunch shelter for the guided hikers, and re-enters the bush for a spell until it breaks out briefly in the open scrub of Hidden Lake. A short side track curves off to the left to the small lake that is accented by a towering waterfall on the far side.

The track moves on into a flat section of the canyon called the Prairie where on a clear day views of Mt Fisher (2131 metres) to the west and Mackinnon Pass to the north become visible. It re-enters the forest again and begins a rocky climb to the deluxe Pompolona Hut, the second night layover for THC hikers. The track crosses a swing bridge over the Pompolona Creek and continues its course up a winding path through low scrub. The track begins to ascend more steeply as it passes a side trail to Quintin Falls and gradually works its way up to Lake Mintaro and then the Mintaro Hut a short distance beyond. If the weather is clear, it can be a good idea to drop your gear here and continue to the pass to be assured of seeing the impressive views without hindrance of clouds or rain. The pass is a 1½ to two-hour walk from the hut and offers a spectacular show during sunset on a clear day.

Accommodation: Mintaro Hut, 24 bunks.

Time: 3½ hours.

Mintaro to Dumpling Hut

The track leaves the hut, swings east with the valley and resumes its climb toward Mackinnon Pass. It crosses the Clinton River a second time and begins to follow a series of switchbacks out of the bush and into the alpine sections of the route. After four km at a knee-bending slant, it reaches the memorial cairn that was built to honour the discovery of the pass by Quintin Mackinnon and Ernest Mitchell in 1888.

The track now levels out and crosses the rest of the alpine region of the pass with impressive views all around the Clinton and Arthur valleys and several nearby peaks. The two most prominent peaks on the pass are Mt Hart (1783 metres) and Mt Balloon (1853 metres) situated right behind the emergency shelter. If the weather is fair, the pass is one place where trampers like to spend some extra time wandering. If it isn't, then they can't get off it fast enough.

The track passes several bog ponds and reaches the emergency shelter where it swings north for the descent. From the pass to Quintin Hut, the track drops 870 metres in a distance of seven km. The rapid descent demands several rest periods for the backs of the legs, and the views are an added reason to linger. Soon the track arrives at Roaring Burn Stream, crosses it and re-enters the bush. Inside the bushline, the track passes Crow's Nest, an emergency shelter for THC trips, and then continues on toward Quintin Hut.

Just past the 19-mile signpost the track arrives at the junction to Quintin Hut where there is an airstrip and several buildings for the guided trampers and a day-use shelter for freedom walkers. One option, if the time can be spared, is to drop the packs and hike the side trail from Quintin to the foot of Sutherland Falls. The falls, three leaps totalling 580 metres, are an impressive sight and often the highlight of the trip for many. Trampers can also wait until the following day, hike an hour back up the track from Dumpling Hut and catch the falls during sunrise, a colourful scene with the early morning sunlight reflecting off the spray and water.

The track leaves Quintin Hut and descends Gentle Annie Hill, re-entering the thick rain forest which is often slippery and wet. It swings north-east and opens up into Arthur Valley as Dumpling Hill moves into sight. The hut is located on the opposite flat and is usually a welcome sight after the long day over the pass.

Accommodation: Dumpling Hut, 24 bunks.

Time: 5½ hours.

Dumpling Hut to Sandfly Point

The track descends back into forest from Dumpling Hut and quickly the Arthur River dominates the air with its roar as the trail closely follows its eastern bank. A little less than two hours from Dumpling, the track reaches Boatshed and then crosses the Arthur on a swing bridge as the river winds to the east. A short distance from the boatshed, the track arrives at the junction with the side trail to Mackay Falls and Bell Rock. Both natural wonders are a short walk from the main track and worth the time to see them, especially the unique Bell Rock where water has eroded a space underneath the rock large enough to stand in.

The track begins to climb a rock shoulder of the valley above Lake Ada where at the high point a view of the lake to the valley of Joe's River can be seen. Then it descends to Giant Gate Falls, passes the falls by a swing bridge and continues to follow the lake shore. Gradually it follows the lake past Doughboy Shelter, a THC hut, and returns to the Arthur River. In the final part of the trip, the track moves through wide open sections of the valley before arriving at Sandfly Point where there is a shelter for those who want to rest their feet before the boat launch across the Milford Sound.

Though it is important to be on time to meet the boat at 2 pm or 4 pm, Sandfly Point is not a place to spend an afternoon. The place is literally a haven for the insect that was it was so rightfully named after.

Time: 5½ hours.

HOLLYFORD TRACK

The following description covers the Hollyford Track from the road to Martins Bay, a trip that can be covered in four days. For those who want to make the trip a circular route, it is possible to continue on from Martins Bay to the mouth of the Awarua River and then cut across east to the head of the Pyke River. From here there is a route along an old cattle track following the Pyke to Lake Alabaster and eventually back to to the Hollyford Track. The trip would demand no less than 10 days if the hikers are in shape and experienced. The circular Hollyford trip is a hard one with much of the track poorly marked. The only hut is at the junction of the Olivine and Pyke rivers (six bunks).

Lower Hollyford Rd to Hidden Falls

From the road's end the old track runs from Humboldt to Swamp Creek close to the river's edge and is subject to considerable flooding during bad weather. In 1980, a new all-weather track was constructed along the bluff with swing bridges over Eel and Swamp creeks, high above the flood level. Either way, the tracks cut through the dense bush of the Hollyford Valley, arrive on the north side of Swamp Creek and quickly introduce trampers to hookgrass. This week leaves its barbs on legs or trousers when bushed against and can cause a hair-raising experience when you pull them off bare skin at night.

Past Swamp Creek the track swings to the east and leaves the river's edge, winds through lush bush and then emerges on the open flat of Hidden Falls Creek where the hut is located five minutes past the bridge. At the bridge a side trail follows the south shore of the creek for a short distance before arriving unexpectedly at the falls.

For those who started at the road's end, it might be worthwhile to push on to the Lake Alabaster Hut, another 3½ hours along the track. For those who had to walk the extra eight km along the road from Gunn's Camp, the Hidden Falls Hut might be too inviting to pass up.

Accommodation: Hidden Falls Hut, 12 bunks.

Time: three hours

Hidden Falls to Lake Alabaster

The track departs from behind the hut and continues through forest before ascending up to its highest point at Little Home Saddle (168 metres). Many sections of the track are carved deeply into clay with streams running through, making the walking a bit slippery and, at times, challenging. On the saddle the forest opens up and for the first time you see the grandeur of Mt Tutoko (2746 metres) and the glaciers clinging to its side.

The track descends steeply from the saddle until it reaches Homer Creek and Little Homer Falls, thundering down 60 metres to the stream. A short distance beyond, or about a 30-minute walk, the track swings back to the Hollyford and crosses Rainbow Stream. The track stays with the river for a distance and then swings away again to a clearing on the lower Pyke where private huts are passed.

After five minutes the track passes the giant swing bridge over the Pyke River and then continues on to the lower end of Lake Alabaster and the park hut.

Accommodation: Lake Alabaster Hut, 12 bunks

Time: 3½ hours

Lake Alabaster to Lake McKerrow

The trail backtracks to the swing bridge over the Pyke, crosses it and then continues beneath the rocky bluffs along the lower section of the river. Here it enters heavy forest where all sight and sound of the two great rivers is lost in the thick canopy of the trees. For two hours the track works its way through the lush bush before breaking out into a clearing next to the Hollyford River, now twice as powerful than it was above the Pyke River junction.

Before reaching Lake McKerrow, the river swings west; a dry river bed, which can usually be easily forded, runs through to the lake on the eastern side. Trampers can cross this channel and walk along the beach on the northern shore of the island to reach the Lake McKerrow Hut, a pleasant hut near the mouth of the main channel, hidden slightly in the bush. If the rains have been heavy, it may be impossible to cross the eastern channel in which case trampers can stay at Demon Trail Hut an hour further up the main trail. One of the best fishing spots for trout is said to be at the mouth of the main channel a few metres from where it empties into Lake McKerrow. Check the intentions book for the most recent catches.

Accommodation: Lake McKerrow Hut, 12 bunks; Demon Trail Hut, 12 bunks.

Time: four hours to McKerrow Hut, 4½ hours to Demon Trail Hut.

Lake McKerrow to Hokuri

The section of track around the eastern shore of Lake McKerrow is named the Demon Trail and for good reason. It has to be the most exhausting non-alpine track in New Zealand. The track, though well defined, climbs up and down one ridge after another with little to look at beyond the incredibly thick bush and forest. Many trampers are more than willing to depart with the small fee that it takes to catch a ride up the lake on a jet-boat run by Hollyford Tourist and Travel.

Starting from Demon Trail Hut, the track swings deep into the bush, climbs and then descends in a pattern that will become all too familiar by the end of the day. It crosses several streams along the way where the water level during flooding might force the use of wire walks. Several times the trail dips down to a beach for a break from the bush and a quick glance of the lake. At Slip Creek, considered the halfway point, there is a rock bivouac nearby large enough to hold six people in case emergency shelter is needed. Most trampers, however, to try to cover the 12 km to Hokuri Hut as fast as possible. Finally the track descends to the lakeshore and the new hut located before Hokuri Stream.

Accommodation: Hokuri Hut, 12 bunks.

Time: 4½ hours.

Hokuri to Martins Bay

The track departs from the hut, travels along the lakeshore for a distance and reaches Hokuri Creek, where there is a wire crossing ten minutes upstream in case of flooding. The track continues along the lake shore for an hour and a half from the hut and passes the site of the township of Jamestown, though little remains of the settlement today.

Another 30 minutes and the track departs from the lake, works its way inland through bush and eventually comes to a clearing and the airstrip of Martins Bay. The huts at the south end of the airstrip are private. The track continues past the end of the grass runway and onward to the mouth of the Hollyford River, passing Jerusalem Creek. From here it works along the bay, passing some artistic rock formations, and eventually arrives at a break in the bush. The track swings to the north between large rock formations and the hut is just beyond these in a small clearing.

Adjacent to the hut is a rocky point with easy access to deep pools loaded with blue cod. Further down the coast is Long Reef and its thriving seal colony. One may also spot penguins along the shore as they shuffle from under one boulder to another. An old cattle track continues north of Long Reef and is the trail to take to Big Bay and the circular route back to the Hollyford River.

Accommodation: Martins Bay Hut, 12 bunks.

Time: 3½ hours.

LAKE HAUROKO—SUPPER COVE—WEST ARM

The following trip takes a minimum of eight days if weather permits hiking every day. The weather in the southern portion of Fiordland can be exceptionally unpredictable and stormy at times. Every party should allow an extra day or two in case of foul weather or flooding forces a delay in the trip.

Lake Hauroko to Halfway Hut

The track leaves the Hauroko Burn Hut at the head of the lake and works its way along the west bank of the Hauroko Burn Stream, passing several deep pools that would delight any fisherman. A few km from the lake, the track crosses a small stream by a wire walk and then begins climbing, eventually rising 150 metres and allowing trampers to see the spray from Hauroko Falls above the trees.

The track descends to the river and crosses it for the first time over a wire walk just below the junction with Gardner Burn. Most river crossings on this trip can be easily forded during fair weather, but if flooding has occurred the wire walks should be used. The track resumes its climb on the canyon wall for a spell then drops back gently to the river before passing a small clearing. From here the track continues to a second, larger clearing where Halfway Hut is located at the south end.

Accommodation: Halfway Hut, 12 bunks.

Time: five hours.

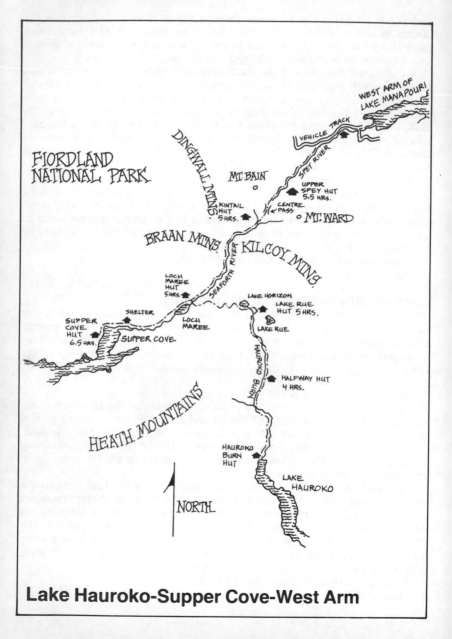

Lake Hauroko-Supper Cove-West Arm

Halfway Hut to Lake Roe

The track returns to the bush at the fringe of the clearing, swings away from the river and crosses another wire over a small stream. It follows a low ridge and gradually works its way back to the river before crossing the Hauroko Burn the second time. If the water level is high, a nearby fallen log serves as a convenient bridge.

The track continues along the west bank, climbing until it reaches a tussock clearing. Stone cairns and metal standards replace the developed trail and lead to Lake Roe where the hut is next to a stand of beech trees 100 metres west of the lake. This is one place where an extra day should be spent exploring the surrounding area. The ridges and rolling tops that circle the lake are filled with pleasant tussock meadows and offer spectacular views of nearby mountain peaks and the entire length of Dusky Sound. The alpine meadows, springy to walk on, are highlighted with rough rock outcrops and a wealth of brown tarns.

Accommodation: Lake Roe Hut, 12 bunks.

Time: five hours.

Lake Roe to Lock Maree

The track leaves the hut and is again marked by metal standards as it climbs a ridge to the west and then skirts the south shore of Lake Horizon. The track passes the lake, swings left and continues climbing until it reaches the top of Pleasant Range. From here another postcard view suddenly materializes of the entire Dusky Sound, from Supper Cover to Resolution Island, with the haze of the open sea beyond.

The track leaves the ridge and begins its drop to the Seaforth River, a 1000-metre descent that seems almost vertical in some spots. For most this is the hardest section of the trip to Supper Cove and is just endured until the track arrives at the river at the top of Loch Maree. The Seaforth can be forded in fair weather, but has been known to rise five metres after a single rain, covering the wire walk and taking several days to fall. In such times, there is little one can do but wait it out. The Loch Maree Hut is located only a few minutes past the river on the north edge of the lake.

Accommodation: Loch Maree Hut, 12 bunks.

Time: five hours.

Loch Maree to Supper Cove

Trampers should be careful when continuing around Loch Maree as heavy rain can make it impassable for a day or so. The lake is a result of comparatively recent landslide activity, and fallen tree trunks still decorate the surrounding area. The track leaves the hut and climbs above the north shore, arriving at perpendicular cliffs on the foot of the lake. There is a wire bolted in the side to help trampers edge around the bluff.

Past Loch Maree, the track descends to Bishop Burn, crosses it on a wire walk and then swings into the original trail that was carved out in 1903 by the Public Works Department. The beginning of the Seaforth is pleasant tramping with an easy descent. The tramper is also aided considerably with a wire walk over Macfarlane and a cable ladder over a cliff. In less than five hours, the track passes the old mariner's refuge, located one km from the mouth of the Seaforth. The hut was constructed in 1903, reconditioned by the park authorities in 1955 and today serves as adequate shelter.

It takes another hour or so to reach the new park hut at Supper Cove as the track climbs up and around the hillside and over some difficult terrain. An alternative is to wait for low tide and follow the sandy beach to the hut. There is a small boat shelter near the hut with a dinghy for public use. The area offers good fishing with blue cod from the shore and groper in the sound.

Accommodation: Old Mariner's Shelter, no bunks; Supper Cove Hut, 14 bunks.

Time: 6½ hours.

Supper Cove to Loch Maree

The description of the track from Supper Cove back to Loch Maree is just a reverse of the previous section, but allow more time for the trip as you will be ascending the Seaforth Valley toward Loch Maree.

Accommodation: Loch Maree Hut, 12 bunks.

Time: seven hours.

Loch Maree to Kintail Hut

The track departs north and follows the western bank of the Seaforth through a flat valley where the tramping is pleasant and the views of the surrounding mountains scenic. Two hours from the hut, the track crosses a small stream by a wire walk and continues through the valley at an easy grade.

The track crosses a second wire at Kenneth Burn Stream and begins its ascent of a gorge towards Gair Loch. The trail climbs out of the gorge, levels out in the valley and passes Gair Loch. From here it is a short distance to the Kintail Hut, located just past the wire walk on the western bank of the Seaforth River, now a mountain stream. The hut is relatively new as it was constructed in 1976 in memory of Lachlan Watson.

Accommodation: Kintail Hut, 12 bunks.

Time: five hours.

Kintail Hut to Upper Spey

The track leaves the hut and soon crosses the Seaforth on a wire walk. It swings east through heavy bush towards Kintail Stream briefly before turning north and beginning its steep climb toward Centre pass. Three other passes, Pillans to the east and Murrells and Mackenzie to the west, can be used and were before Centre Pass was developed in the late 1970s. Centre Pass is an easier route, however, as it is much more direct and a shorter crossing between the Seaforth and Spey valleys.

The track leaves the bush and continues its steep ascent toward the pass where it becomes more of a route marked by metal standards. The pass is a good place to take an extended rest after the tough climb as it offers unique views of Tripod Hill across from Gair Loch in the Seaforth Valley. The descent to the east is not quite as steep as the climb to the pass and soon the track comes to the Warren Burn Stream, the true headwaters of the Spey River. It continues along the eastern bank of the stream as it descends into the Spey Valley.

Eventually the track re-enters the bush and arrives at a large clearing along the Warren Burn with the Upper Spey Hut located at the southern end.

Accommodation: Upper Spey Hut, 12 bunks.

Time: five hours.

Upper Spey to West Arm

The track cuts through the large clearing, leaving the hut behind and re-entering the bush at the north end. It crosses over to the western bank of the Spey on a wire walk just before reaching Waterfall Creek. From here the track fords the small Waterfall Creek and continues through Spey Valley, now open ribbonwood countryside. Staying close to the river's edge, the track passes the junction to Diamond Creek and Short Stream before arriving at a wire walk across Dashwood Stream.

The track becomes a well-developed trail after Dashwood Stream as it was part of the old Doubtful Sound Walking Track at one time. Eventually it climbs up to the Wilmot Pass Rd and follows the road north for 20 minutes to arrive at Mica Burn Hut. This would be the place to stay if overnight accommodation is needed before the launch trip back across Lake Manapouri. From the hut it is another 30 minutes to the West Arm of the lake where Fiordland Travel cruise boats pick up or drop off trampers.

Accommodation: Mica Burn Hut, 12 bunks.

Time: five hours.

Stewart Island

Round-the-Island Track

Going to Stewart Island is going to extremes in New Zealand. The island is the southernmost point of the country, located off the South Island, below Invercargill. It is the most remote area with only one small village, 400 residents and vast tracts of wilderness that rarely feel the imprint of a hiking boot. It has the most unpredictable weather in its skies, the most birdlife in its trees and unquestionably the most mud on its tracks.

In a country of out-of-the-way places, Stewart Island is the most out of the way. It takes a special effort to get there, special gear to endure it and a special person to appreciate it. In short, a tramper and a backpack.

The island covers 1680 sq km and measures 65 km from north to south and 40 km from east to west. But its real beauty lies in its 755 km of coastline, which includes numerous sandy beaches, crystal clear bays and half-hidden inlets. The interior is mostly bushclad and generally broken up by steep gullies with several ridges emerging above the bushline. The highest point on Stewart Island is Mt Anglem, only 976 metres, but much of the backcountry is as rugged as mountains tracts in the North or South Islands.

The island's main attractions are the unusual geological structures — rounded granite tops, weathered rock formations and extensive sand dunes — combined with a fine selection of New Zealand's native birdlife; most trampers are in awe of the island and appreciative of its isolation. Time slows down and almost stops for the land, the small village of Oban and the permanent residents of Stewart Island. Visitors find life simpler, the pace slower and a relaxed atmosphere surrounding the village and the people. Trampers find it a delight in comparison with the busy, heavily used tracks of the South Island. The non-commercialized nature of Stewart Island, where the huts are small and the tracks generally uncrowded and undevel-

A   Martins Bay, at the end of the Hollyford Track
B   A member of the seal colony at Martins Bay

oped, is a welcome change to most hikers.

The island has over 220 km of tracks maintained by the New Zealand Forest Service, including a seven-day circular route in the northern section and a dozen day walks out of Halfmoon Bay. For the overnight trek, there are a number of tracks from which one can choose. Surprisingly, though, of the 5000 trampers who visit the island every year, only 15% hike beyond Christmas Village Bay, so most of the backcountry is left to the handful that are willing to endure the longer journey and a little mud.

Tramping on Stewart is not easy. Most tracks outside the Halfmoon Bay area, including the route described in this chapter, are rated strenuous and should be attempted only by well-equipped and well-prepared parties. You encounter mud only a few km from the village and have it to deal with almost the entire trip, whether rain or shine. It is impossible to avoid. Most trampers give up the battle after the first day and slosh through it from then on, ending each evening with a communal washing of boots, socks and feet. It varies from ankle deep in many places to knee deep in some ill-famed spots such as Chocolate Swamp or the trail to Mt Anglem. Gaiters are a good piece of equipment to have but generally, if you are planning extensive hikes on the island, you just have to get used to wet socks, mud-splattered pants and boots that will never be the same colour again.

The gullies and ridges also make the tramping hard as the tracks are constantly going either up or down and rarely it seems, in a straight path. Though not as towering as the Southern Alps, Stewart Island is just as hard on the knees as a walk through Arthur's Pass National Park. Because of this, most hikers tend to undersize the island or the length of the walk in front of them. The mud and ridges will slow you down considerably from your normal speed. When you mix the two together it almost becomes comical. Many times you will end up sliding down steep sections of the track on your behind with ankle-deep mud oozing up between your legs. Like the sandflies of the Milford Sound, this is something you get used to, if that seems possible.

The weather also plays havoc with trampers. The overall climate of Stewart Island is surprisingly mild, considering its latitude. Temperatures are pleasant most of the year while heavy frost is extremely rare in the winter. Annual rainfall at Halfmoon Bay is approximately 1600 mm and over 5000 mm in the hill country in the south and west. The daily weather,

A A Mud! Stewart Island
B B Murray Beach on the way to Christmas Village, Stewart
    Island

or better yet the hourly weather, is another story. It is not uncommon for it to be raining one hour, sunny the next and raining again within an hour of the first shower. The day-to-day weather is the most unpredictable in New Zealand and trampers quickly learn to keep their rain gear within easy reach. It can and does rain any day of the year and many times rain is accompanied by strong westerly winds. Snow is rare except on some of the peaks.

For putting up with the mud, hilly terrain and indecisive weather, the tramper is amply rewarded. The forests and vegetation are unique. Beech, the tree that dominates the rest of New Zealand is absent from Stewart Island. The predominant lowland flora is podocarp-hardwood forest with exceptionally tall rimu, miro, totara and kamahi forming the canopy. Due to the mild winters, rainfall and porous soil, most of the island is heavily forested, held together by vines and carpeted in ferns. So lush, thick and green, the vegetation at times appears to be choking the track.

The scrub is also thick at the sub-alpine regions above the bushline while in the Freshwater and Rukeahua river valleys the land, made up of bog and heath vegetation, is windswept and low lying. This causes more than just damp tramping. It has been the inspiration behind killer-mud-pond-horror stories spreading on the island.

If the vegetation and forests are unique, the birdlife is exceptional. The island is known for its large and diverse bird populations that have survived many of the ecological disasters of the mainland. Rats, cats and opossums have greatly affected the once thriving species, but their numbers and variety are still greater than anywhere else in the country.

Kiwi watchers have one of the best chances to see the national bird as it resides throughout Stewart Island and in particularly strong numbers around Mason Bay and areas south of Paterson Inlet. Bush birds such as bellbirds, tuis, wood pigeons and fantails exist plentifully on most of the island, while parakeets and kaka (forest parrot), rare on the mainland, can be spotted often in the bush. Stewart Island is also the home of several species of penguins, Whiteface Heron and the extremely rare kakapo, a flightless parrot.

Even if you are not a binocular-carrying bird watcher, you can't help noticing their presence. Tramping in Stewart Island is like having constant stereophonic music on the tracks. Their whistles and songs can be heard from dawn to dusk, from one end of the trail to the other. It might just be the sweetest singing in New Zealand.

Other wildlife on the island, all introduced, are red and whitetail deer, rats, domestic cats that have gone wild, and opossums, which have caused considerable destruction on the north coast by their numbers and habit of stripping trees to death. Nine whitetail deer were liberated at Port Pegasus in 1908 and since have scattered throughout the region. The animal is known for its extremely good sense of sight, smell and hearing and has become a prized trophy for hunters because of the difficulty in stalking it.

On Stewart Island they are commonly known as 'little grey ghosts' and can be seen occasionally playing on the beach early in the morning.

Trampers too find a playground on the beaches which are uncrowded, unspoiled and a welcome sight after a day in the mud. The trek up the east coast to Christmas Village includes seven major stretches of sand and surf with Murray Beach being the largest and most spectacular. Beachcombing, shell collecting and mussel and paua gathering are common activities on most of them. The largest beach on Stewart Island is the impressive Mason Bay, a 14-km beach on the west coast characterized by its extensive sand dunes. The beach is noted for excellent shell scavenging and an occasional stranded whale, but it can be a particularly moving sight any time with the surf breaking hundreds of metres out and roaring onto the hard sand beach.

HISTORY

The Maoris had a legend for the creation of Stewart Island. They contended that a young man named Maui left the Polynesian Islands to go fishing. He paddled far into the sea and, far out of sight of his homeland, dropped anchor. In time his canoe became the South Island, a great fish he caught became the North Island and his anchor was Stewart Island, holding everything in place.

Excavations in the area haven't turned up anything of Maui or his giant fish but they have provided evidence that as early as early as the 13th century, tribes of Polynesian origin migrated to the island to hunt moa birds. Maori settlement was scarce, however, because of the inability to grow kumara (sweet potato), the main food of settlements of the north. Southern Maoris were more nomadic and never settled on Stewart Island in great numbers. They did make annual migrations to the outer islands seeking muttonbird, a favourite food, and to the main island searching out eel, shellfish and certain birds. At the time of the first European contact the main settlement was at Ruapuke Island with smaller groups at Port Williams, the Neck and Port Adventure. The islands were mainly a haven for peaceful Maoris who wanted to avoid the tribal wars on the mainland.

The first European to sight the area was Captain Cook in the *Endeavour* in 1770 but he left confused as to whether it was an island or part of the South Island. Cook finally decided it was part of the South Island, labelling it Cape South. There is evidence that American sealer O F Smith had discovered Foveaux Strait in 1804 for it was known briefly as Smith's Strait, but during the sealing boom a few years later it picked up its present name for a governor of New South Wales. The island derived its name from William Stewart, the first officer of the English sealer *Pegasus*. Stewart charted large sections of the coast during a sealing trip in 1809, to draft the first detailed map of the island. He also had them published seven years later, permanently imprinting his name on the region.

There is confusion as to who was the first European to land on the island, but by the early 1800s sealers were staying for months at a time to collect skins for their mother ship. In 1825, a group of sealers and their Maori wives set up a permanent settlement on Codfish Island as their industry pulled a trickle of humanity to the area. Sealing was finished by the late 1820s and whaling replaced it temporarily. Stewart Island was a port of call for whalers since the early 1800s as a place of rest after a season at the whaling bases. There were also small whaling bases on the island but this industry never really turned a profit and contributed to the island's progress.

Neither did timber. Though the island was almost completely covered with bush and forest, most of it was not millable and little was profitably accessible. Still the first mill on a commercial basis opened up at Kaipipi Bay in 1861 while another was established in Halfmoon Bay in 1874 in an area now named Mill Creek. Both stimulated the growth of the island to a small degree until the timber industry elapsed in 1931 when the last remaining mill on Maori Beach closed down.

It was gold and later tin that brought people and progress to this remote area of New Zealand. In 1886 gold was discovered at Port William in the wake of the great Otago and West Coast gold rushes. A small-scale rush resulted and further strikes were made at a few of the beaches on the north and west coast. The greatest output was between 1889 and 1894 when, ironically, the tin operations in the ranges above Port Pegasus turned out fair quantities of gold.

The only enterprise that has proved to be enduring throughout the years is fishing. Initially fishermen were few in numbers and were handicapped by the lack of regular transport to Stewart Island from the mainland. But when a steamer service from Bluff began in 1885, the industry grew significantly, resulting in the construction of cleaning sheds on Ruapuke Island.

Marketable fish filled the seas around the island and the local fleet grew large enough to warrant a refrigeration plant, built in the North Arm of Port Pegasus in 1897. Today fishing is the major occupation with most of the 400 residents involved in it one way or another. The main catch is crayfish from June to January for export trade while blue cod and paua are taken for the New Zealand market.

Oysters also supplied an income for a short time when Europeans began working the beds near Port Adventure in the early 1860s. Unquestionably, the local Maoris had already discovered the ready food supply and between the two groups the beds were almost worked out by 1867. Extensive deep beds off Port William met the same fate in four years and when beds out from Halfmoon Bay began showing signs of exhaustion in 1877 the government stepped in. A closed season was declared and research followed in an effort to keep the beds more or less at the same level. Gradually the industry, working beds in a wide area of Foveaux Strait, moved its base of operations to Bluff and has little to do with Stewart Island today.

The only other industry to survive the past is muttonbirding. As direct result of the Deed of Cession signed in 1864, only descendants of the original Maori owners of Rakiura are allowed to search and take muttonbirds from the island. Even today the only Europeans allowed this privilege are husbands or wives of legitimate birders.

The Sooty Petrel, known affectionately as the muttonbird, nests in burrows on the headland and islets of the Stewart Island region, laying eggs in November and hatching them towards the end of December. The parents stay with the chicks for three months and then depart on their annual migration in March. It is at this stage that the Maoris search out and kill the young left to fend for themselves. The remaining chicks will depart in May to follow their parents after they have become proficient in flight.

Although considered by many visitors as greasy, muttonbirds are viewed as a great delicacy by the Maoris. It is the annual hunt, however, that has great significance with this segment of New Zealand's population. Mutton-birding may be the only Maori custom to have successfully withstood the assault of European culture and exploitation, a rare thing today.

GETTING STARTED

There is only one way to get to Stewart Island, across the Foveaux Strait, but several ways of doing it. All involve passing through Invercargill first.

Most trampers will take the ferry, *MV Wairua*, from Bluff out to the island. The vessel runs throughout the year with two or three sailings a week depending on the season. Taking the ferry across the strait can be an adventure in itself. If the weather is calm, the ride will be an extremely pleasant cruise with the possibility of seeing several species of rare birds. If the conditions are poor, you may have trouble hanging on to your seat and your breakfast. Often called the roughest crossing in the world, the strait tosses the ship from side to side, breaking waves over the gunwale and leaving the locals nodding and the visitors horrified.

The boat operates during the summer on Monday, Wednesday and Friday. The crossing takes about 2½ hours, depending on the conditions. You can easily hike to the first hut at Port William or the North Arm the day you arrive on the island. On the return, the ferry leaves late enough for trampers to hike in and catch the sailing. H&H Motors has a bus that leaves Invercargill from the corner of Don and Kelvin Sts and connects with the ferry at Bluff, as well as having a bus to meet all ferries arriving at the mainland.

You can also fly to the island with Southern Air, which has three flights a day during the summer and two in the winter. The flight takes about 20 minutes and on a nice day offers spectacular views of Bluff Harbour, Muttonbird Islands and the eastern coastline where most people end up hiking. On a poor day, you may simply not fly and it's not uncommon to wait a day or two for a flight. The ferry, on the other hand, goes rain, shine, hurricane or monsoon. Cheaper airfares can be obtained by flying stand-by but you have to be at the Invercargill airport 15 minutes before departure to see if any of the twelve seats are available. Youth hostel members get a discount on top of the stand-by fare, making the flight only a few dollars more than the ferry. Southern Air will charge you for excess weight and most backpacks tend to be over.

Once stepping ashore, you will find Oban is a village of only 250 buildings of which almost half are holiday cottages. There is a general store at the foot of the ferry dock but it is usually more practical and cheaper to outfit your trip in Invercargill. The local supply of backpacker's food — dried fruit, nuts, one-pot meals — can be very limited at times as well as costly. The town also has a cafe, post office and a bar, often filled with local colour. Accommodation inlcudes two hotel/motels, cabin and campsites (Horseshoe Haven) and a few guest houses and dormitory living situations run by locals seeking an extra income in the summer. The last two tend to change occasionally and it is best to stop at the NZFS office for the latest list of boarders in Oban. Some can be a real bargain.

The first stop for all trampers should be the NZFS office on Main St, two blocks from the ferry. If you are planning to spend the night in town, two a list of the latest accommodation will be available. If you want to hit the trail immediately, the chief ranger can point you in the right direction and give you a reassuring push, along with some good tips. Maps and track guides are available, as are booklets about the birdlife and flora. Most importantly, the ranger can give you solid information about the trip you have selected or help choose a track to undertake. All trampers should sign the intentions book at the office before departing on any trek, and also sign out on their return.

There is a wide variety of backcountry trips to choose from but most trampers usually hike to Port William the first night, Big Bungaree the second and possibly Christmas Village the third. On the fourth day they turn around and head back to Oban to complete their five or six-day adventure. This section is by far the best, much of it boarded, and has some of the most scenic areas of the island. You will encounter mud, but not the amount that should alarm anybody. Some trampers continue past Christmas Village, around the north coast to the west coast and then cut across to Oban by way of Ruggedy Flats and Freshwater Valley. This trip takes seven or eight days and is considered strenuous, but nothing a well-prepared backpacker couldn't handle. Others wishing to see just Mason Bay hike west of Oban to North Arm the first day, continue to Freshwater hut the second and reach the beach on the third night, returning the same way.

It is possible to cut out much back-tracking by hiring the services of a local boatee or fisherman to take you part of the way up the coast. Many will drop you off at any of the first three huts north of Oban or to the North Arm west towards Mason Bay. Inquire at the NZFS office or the general stores.

If you arrive during the Christmas season, it might pay to bring a tent. The Port William hut is new, holds 30 bunks and is very deluxe, but everything after that is just the opposite with many of the huts holding only four or six trampers. Other good items to take along are gaiters, a trusted rain parka and a pair of socks you might not mind tossing away after the hike. Those who are taking the longer circular routes should double check their food supplies and make sure they have sufficient. It may hurt your shoulders the first day to carry extra food, but your stomach will be thankful on the last. It is also wise to allow an extra day for either miserable weather or memorable lingering on an isolated beach. Maps to use are NZMS 219, the Lands or Survey recreation map of Stewart Island, or series one S185, S186 and S189 for better detail.

ROUND THE ISLAND
The trip described is a 10-day trek to Mason Bay, beginning and ending at Oban. Those who have only seven days can pass up Mason Bay and save three days by hiking from Benson Peak (Upper Freshwater Hut) to Freshwater Landing and then over to North Arm the following day and finally into Oban.

Halfmoon Bay to Port William
The first five km of the hike is the road to Lee Bay which begins by the general store. It goes over a series of hills to Horseshoe Bay and one final one to Lee Bay. The track crosses a swing bridge at Little River and resumes in a tidal area where it is easy to get wrong-routed. From Little River it is a hour to Maori Beach, where the track descends and follows the smooth, sandy beach to a swing bridge at the far end. After crossing the stream, the track leaves the beach and climbs through a hilly section before descending to Port William on the other side of the headland. A wharf can be seen in the distance and the hut is only a short distance beyond. It is possible at low tide to walk along the coast for the last section instead of tramping up and down every hill from Maori Beach to the hut.

Port William is the nicest hut on the island and during the summer the most heavily used. For those who want to save a day or avoid a crowd, it is only a three-hour hike to the next hut at Big Bungaree.

Accommodation: Port William Hut, 30 bunks.

Time: four hours.

Port William to Big Bungaree
The ooze on the first day was nothing. This is where the mud begins. The track starts at the grassy clearing on the other side of the wharf and climbs quickly into the hill country, high above the sea with impressive views an hour after leaving the hut. But after no more than 20 minutes on the track, the slipping and sliding up one hill and down the next begins. The track reaches a high point where there is a scenic view of Muttonbird Islands and then begins a steady drop to Little Bungaree Beach. It crosses one more headland before descending to Big Bungaree Beach and then follows the beach to the hut at the far end. For those with time on their hands, this is a place worth an extra day.

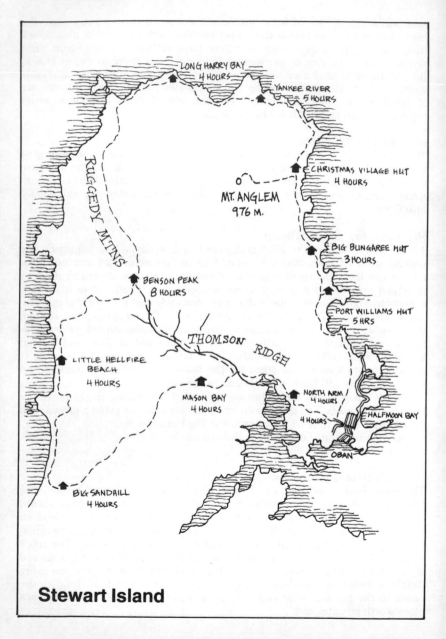

Stewart Island

Accommodation: Big Bungaree Hut, 12 bunks
Time: three hours

Big Bungaree to Christmas Village

The track begins climbing again and then follows a series of hills as it works its way inland from Gull Rock Point. After an hour of climbing up and down, the track descends sharply onto Murray Beach, catching most trampers unprepared for the beautiful stretch of golden sand. Here is a good spot for a swim, shell collecting, mussel or paua hunting or, as one member of my expedition did, a nude run to the end. Anything but sunbathing as the sandflies will quickly drive anyone into the water or back into their clothes.

At the far end of the beach, the track begins again and crosses Murray Stream to follow an old tramline for a distance before entering virgin forest. The track resumes its up and down climb of hills, crosses several streams and branches just before reaching Christmas Village. The right fork leads to the hut and then re-enters the bush to join up with the main route. If the hut is full, there is a grassy spot a few yards down the trail towards the beach that can be used to set up a tent or lean-to.

Accommodation: Christmas Village Hut, six bunks.

Time: four hours on a nice day.

Christmas Village to Yankee River

At this point most trampers turn around and head back. Some spend an extra day at Christmas Village to climb Mt Anglem, the highest point in the area and a place for spectacular views of the South Island and most of Stewart Island. The junction for the track to the summit is reached in about 20 minutes along the main route to Yankee River and the entire round trip takes about six hours. The mud on this side trail can be exceptionally bad at times.

For those who are now used to the brown goop, don't mind a few swamps and can endure an occasional long and boring stretch, the route around the island can offer pleasures to trampers few other areas in New Zealand can. The most obvious, of course, is the peace and tranquility of seeing few people, if any at all, in the remainder of the trip. This can lead to a more frequent observation of the natural wildlife and a feeling of solitude that is rare in today's world.

From a signpost below the hut, the track crosses a creek and then climbs steeply (what else?) over a short ridge where it joins the main northern trail. It descends to a large creek, crosses by a swing bridge, and arrives at the junction of the track to Mt Anglem. From here the track works its way through low, thick bush country until it descends on to Lucky Beach. On this stretch the track is unusually dry as the tall rimu tress provide a good canopy.

The track begins again at the west end of Lucky Beach and climbs steadily through dense areas of fern and bush. Be careful in this section as the track can be easily lost when it re-enters the heavily forested region. For the next two hours the track climbs and falls almost the entire way to Yankee River. Just in time and usually greeted with a great sigh of relief, a signpost pops up and points the way to the hut on the river.

Accommodation: Yankee River Hut, 12 bunks.

Time: five hours.

Yankee River to Long Harry Bay

Backtrack to the main trail which crosses the Yankee River by a swing bridge and then rises quite steadily over the ridge of Black Rock Pt before descending to Smoky Beach. The climb is a knee bender and it will take a full two hours to reach the beach, a pleasant spot for a lunchtime break with its unusual sand hills. The track follows the beach and crosses Smoky River at the west end by a swing bridge. From the river to Long Harry Bay, the track crosses a series of ridges and half a dozen streams. Be prepared for slow tramping and a few tough climbs because of the broken nature of the terrain. The track finally descends onto Long Harry Bay two hours after leaving Smoky Beach. The hut is about 150 metres down the beach.

Accommodation: Long Harry Hut, six bunks.

Time: four hours.

Long Harry Bay to Benson Peak

The track continues on the coastal terrace behind the hut for a short distance before climbing along Cave Point Ridge. Good views can be obtained on clear days along the ridge before the track descends to the broken coastline below. The track follows the rugged coast for a spell then re-enters the low-lying scrub at a marked signpost. After a steep climb over a ridge and a three-hour walk from Long Harry Bay, it descends into East Ruggedy Beach.

The track moves inland from the beach, covering sand dune and scrub country until it reaches a small stream. Just beyond is the junction to West Ruggedy Beach. For those who want to break this hike into two days, there is a cave at the north end of West Ruggedy Beach that is suitable accommodation for a small group. The hike to the cave is an hour from East Ruggedy or about 30-40 minutes from the track junction. For those going on to the shelter at Benson Peak take the left-hand fork and be prepared for a further five-hour tramp. The entire hike from Larry Harry Bay to Benson Peak is eight hours and those undertaking it should plan on an early start.

From the end of the sandhills at the junction, the track works its way over to the east side of the Ruggedy Range. Trampers are bound to run into some extremely deep bogs and related mud holes although board walks now span the worst spots. On reaching the range, the track turns south with good views of Red Head Peak to the west and reaches the junction to Waituna Bay. The right-hand fork leads off to the bay on a track that crosses the Ruggedy Range and continues to Mason Bay after Waituna. The other fork goes to Benson Peak, about a two-hour hike. The hut is situated below the peak on the south-east side.

Accommodation: Upper Freshwater Hut, six bunks.

Time: eight hours.

Benson Peak to Little Hellfire Beach

The track leaves the hut and travels through thick native bush and a few open gullies before leading into open tussock areas, a side arm of the Ruggedy Flats. Through the tussock, the track is marked by poles until it enters native scrub again and begins its short and steep climb to Big Sandpass Saddle. Once the track reaches the saddle, it follows the main ridge and then descends sharply towards Richard Point, curving southward and eventually arriving at Little Hellfire Beach after a three-hour tramp from Big Sandpass. The NZFS keeps the track well marked with white tags and poles in the areas of heavy coastal vegetation, but caution should be taken as the thick bush causes slippery hiking at times. A small bivouac shelter which can sleep four is located at the north end of Little Hellfire.

Accommodation: Bivouac, sleeps four.

Time: five hours.

Little Hellfire Beach to Mason Bay

Follow the beach to the south end and pick up the track where it is marked by a signpost. The track quickly moves inland and climbs over a bush saddle around Mason Head before descending onto the north end of the bay. From here you follow the hard sandy beach for one of the most scenic walks on the island and certainly the most rewarding for beachcombers or shell hunters. Mussels are abundant and excellent when steamed with a clove or two of garlic. Paua is also available though many visitors, after cooking it for the first time, would just as soon chew on a rubber inner tube.

The area also has an abundance of sand dunes and unusual rock formations worth an afternoon of exploring. After 45 minutes or so down the beach, a signpost points the way to the Mason Bay hut, a short walk from the beach. Mason Bay continues for another 10 km that makes for an interesting day hike if the time can be spared.

Accommodation: Mason Bay hut, 16 bunks.

Time: four hours.

Mason Bay to North Arm

The track leaves Mason Bay and turns into a tractor path, quickly passing the Island Hill Homestead, one of the two on the west coast. It continues as a tractor path around Island Hill and along the Scott Burn River system or swamp or whatever it is, where a board walk gets you over more mud and bog. After a three-hour walk the track reaches Freshwater River and crosses it to the hut, a good place for lunch.

The track begins again behind the hut and works its way over Thomson Ridge after crossing two small streams, part of the Freshwater River system. The ridge goes above the bushline and the steep track might be wet and slippery at times. Normally the hike from Freshwater to North Arm hut is three hours if the conditions are not perfect, it may take four hours or longer. The track descends Thomson Ridge and gradually makes its way to the North Arm of Paterson Inlet. The hut is located at the north-east corner of the North Arm.

Accommodation: North Arm Hut, 15 bunks.

Time: six hours.

North Arm to Halfmoon Bay

The track follows North Arm for a short distance and then turns east, moving up into scrub vegetation. After turning inland, the track joins up with an old sawmill tramline that leads through regenerating timber and then gradually works its way into coastal bush again. Eventually the track leads into Fern Gully along Mill Creek and then to Kaipipi Rd outside of Oban. The trip takes four hours and trampers planning to catch the afternoon ferry should get an early start from North Arm.

Time: four hours.

Appendixes

APPENDIX A: GUIDING COMPANIES
The following guiding companies offer organized tramping trips into New Zealand's backcountry for those who want to lighten their load or have better accommodation along the track. Most companies maintain their own huts which usually include showers, mattresses and bedding and other luxuries of life. Advance booking is strongly recommended for any trip.

Alpine Guides Ltd
This Mt Cook Company offers guides for a variety of trips that range from a few hours to 10 days in the Southern Alps. The guide services range from glacier ski trips to mountaineering courses; many trampers use them to help with the alpine crossing of the Copland Track. For more information: Alpine Guides Ltd, PO Box 20, Mount Cook.

Dannes Safari
Mostly a rafting company, Dannes offers various rafting-hiking combinations throughout the bush around Queenstown and Mt Aspiring National Park. One guided expedition is a three-day trip that begins at the Dart Glacier and continues down the Dart Valley. For more information: Dannes Safari, PO Box 230, Queenstown.

Hollyford Tourist & Travel Co
This company runs a four-day tour from November to Christmas and then March to the end of April that combines tramping with daily jet boat rides to Martins Bay and back. From Christmas to February the trip is extended to five days with extra time spent at Martins Bay. For more information: Hollyford Tourist & Travel Co Ltd, PO Box 216, Invercargill.

Kaimanawa Tours & Treks
Among the many activities Kaimanawa Tours & Treks offer are guided tramps from two to five days in Kaimanawa State Forest Park. All trips begin and end in Taupo and are customized for parties of two to five hikers at a cost of $40 per person per day. For more information: to Kaimanawa Tours & Treks, PO Box 321, Taupo.

Native Forests Action Council
The council, which has been actively campaigning against logging in New Zealand's native forests, offers a single-day guided walk in Pureora State Forest for $25 per person and an overnight trip into Waihaha Forest for $40. All trips begin and end at Taupo and specialize in flora and bird observation. For more information: Forest Walks, PO Box 142, Taupo.

Routeburn Walk Ltd
For the Routeburn, you can be part of a four-day walk that begins and ends in Queenstown. The season runs from mid-November to the end of April. For more information: Routeburn Walk Ltd, PO Box 271, Queenstown.

Te Rehuwai Safaris
The company offers a five-day trek through the Whakatane River Valley of the Urewera National Park. The cost is $115 (in 1980). The outing features Maori guides well versed in the history and folklore of the area. For more information: Te Rehuwai Safaris, Private Bag, Rotorua.

Tourist Hotel Corporation
This is the government agency that runs the guided Milford Track walk and assists the National Park Service in maintaining the trail. Although THC offers a variety of options, the basic package is five days with three nights on the track in first-class huts and the fourth at the Milford Sound. For reservations or more information: THC Central Reservations Office, PO Box 2207, Auckland.

Venturetreks Ltd
From the end of December to the end of February, Venturetreks offers a five-day tramp in Kaimanawa State Forest Park that begins in Ohakune with a helicopter ride to the centre of the reserve. They also have a five-day Wanganui River Walk which, like the Kaimanawa trip, combines tramping with jet boat rides. For more information: Venturetreks Ltd, PO Box 3839, Auckland.

Waimai Tourist Co
This Christchurch company offers a Heaphy trip with bus and air transport combining to get each party from one end of the track back to Karamea. From there a bus completes the trip to Christchurch. For more information: Waimai Tourist Company, PO Box 2408, Christchurch.

APPENDIX B: OTHER TRACKS & STATE FOREST PARKS

TRACKS: NORTH ISLAND

Cape Reinga-Ninety Mile Beach
Begin along any section of Ninety Mile Beach, which is really only 64 miles (102 km) long, and head north for Cape Reinga, camping along the way. At the north end of the beach is the beginning of the New Zealand Walk-

way to the Cape. From there, continue on to Tapotupotu Bay, a beautifully secluded campground, then along the northern coast to the campground at Spirits Bay. From the bay, there is a road south to Waitiki Landing and public transport. From the end of Ninety Mile Beach to Spirits Bay is a three or four-day trip that can be handled by most trampers. Bring a tent and suntan lotion.

Northern Crossing
This track, which crosses the Tararua State Forest Park, requires three to four days to complete. It begins at the end of Gladstone Rd off of SH 57 and ends at the Waingawa Rd end on the east side. The trek involves considerable travel along mountain ridges but has a series of NZFS huts for trampers to use. The tramp would be a strenuous one.

Waimana Route
This route runs from Maungapohatu north along the Waimana River to the Waimana Valley Rd in Urewera National Park. The trip would require four or five days, a tent and some experience as a backpacker.

Whakatane River Track
Parallel to the Waimana River is the Whakatane River Track which begins north of Ruatahuna and finishes at Ruatoki Rd on the northern tip of Urewera. The track is benched for part of the way at the beginning and the end. The trip requires five days and would be a strenuous one.

Waitakere Ranges
This area, situated between the western edge of Auckland and the Tasman Sea, contains more than 185 km of tracks that criss-cross 10,000 hectares of ancient volcanic grounds. A number of overnight or even three-day tramps can be put together, a favourite being the hike to Whatipu Beach at the southern tip. Heavy traffic on the tracks is possible in the summer as the park is only an hour's drive from Auckland.

Great Barrier Forest
The 28,000-hectare island north of Auckland in the Hauraki Gulf has 28 cut or benched tracks and two huts administered by the NZFS. The island is noted for its rugged coastline, many bays and excellent swimming, snorkeling and coastal fishing. A ferry runs to the island during the summer and there is an NZFS office at Port Fitzroy. A popular area is the track on the west side of Whangaparapara Harbour.

TRACKS: SOUTH ISLAND

Okarito Walk
A two-day tramp down the historical beach south of Okarito, a boom town

during the gold rush. The track is cut, signposted and highlighted by old huts, a gold dredge and other artifacts from the colourful era of the 1860s. Take a tent and insect dope and be prepared to get your feet wet in a few fords. The youth hostel in the old one-room school house serves as good accommodation before or after the mild hike.

Hackett-Pelorus Track
This three-day trip in Mt Richmond State Forest Park begins at Roding River, 27 km from Nelson, and ends at Pelorus River Rd, where a good camping ground is located. The well-marked track has a series of NZFS huts along it. The trip would be medium to strenuous.

Wakamarina-Onamalutu Goldminers Track
Also located in Mt Richmond State Forest Park, the track begins at the end of Wakamarina Rd, 19 km from Canvastown. The trip is mild and would require only two days to cross the range to Wairau Valley.

D'Urville Valley
This valley is harder than Travers or Sabine in Nelson Lakes National Park and thus is not as popular or well used. It begins at the end of Lake Rotoroa where a track leads from D'Urville Hut to the bivouac at the head of the valley. In between there are two park huts and the Moss Pass Track which leads into Sabine River.

Karamea River Track
Start with the Wangapeka Track at Rolling Junction in North-West Nelson State Forest Park and take the eastern fork at the Tabernacle Junction, past Helicopter Flat Hut. This well-marked track follows the Karamea River past several NZFS huts and then up Mt Arthur tableland. Eventually it arrives at the Graham Rd head in the Motueka Valley. The trip from Dart River would take five to seven days.

Shotover River
The track begins at the end of Skipper's Rd, an incredible journey in itself. It winds along the river, fording it many times and connects with Sixteen Mile and Hundred Mile huts. The track ends at the second hut but there is a route that follows Tyndall Creek over Shotover Saddle to West Branch Track and eventually to Wanaka-Mt Aspiring Rd. The entire trip would take four or five days through barren, rocky terrain. The trek, which lies outside Mt Aspiring National Park, would be a strenuous one.

George Sound
A three-day trek from the head of Lake Te Anau's Middle Fiord in Fiordland to George Sound with three huts spaced along the track. Transport (Fiordland Travel) is needed to the head of Middle Fiord, and a dinghy is

available from the park headquarters to cross Lake Hankinson. The trip is generally considered strenuous.

Lake Monowai
A track leads from Monowai in Fiordland to Green Lake and then Clark Hut, requiring nine hours for the walk. Another three hours beyond and the track reaches Monowai Hut. The trip, through scrubby flats, beech forest and tussock flats, is considered medium to strenuous.

Boundary Track
The track begins at the end of the south bay of Lake Hauroko in Fiordland and works through beaches and ridges to Teal Bay Hut. It is eight hours one way along a well-marked and cut trail.

STATE FOREST PARKS: NORTH ISLAND

Kaweka
The park lies west of Hawke's Bay and covers most of the Kaweka Range in its 61,000 hectares. There are 29 huts and bivouacs scattered throughout the area and connected by a series of bush tracks. The weather is generally not as severe as most mountainous areas. Best access is from the south-east corner at Willowford where there is an NZFS office.

Kaimai-Mamaku
A popular place for Auckland and Rotorua trampers, Kaimai-Mamaku stretches north from the Hamilton-Rotorua Highway in a mountainous area that is known for its relatively mild weather. The northern section is the most popular for one or two-day trips. The Waikato Tramping Club maintains huts in the Waiorongomai and Waitengaue valleys. There is easy access from either the western or eastern side of the park.

Ruahine
Not as heavily used as its counterpart Tararua State Forest Park, Ruahine offers the same rugged mountain forests but is less developed. There are huts erected by clubs from Hawke's Bay and Manawatu but the park has never really been the domain of trampers. Bess access is along public roads from the eastern side.

Haurangi
The park, east of Wellington, covers 16,000 hectares of the rugged Aorangi Mountains and has long been a favourite with hunters but not so much with trampers. The area includes attractive bushclad valleys connected by easily negotiable passes and a handful of NZFS huts. Main access roads are Martinborough-Cape Palliser and Martinborough-White Rock.

Pirongia

Located 25 km south of Hamilton, Pirongia covers 13,000 hectares around the slopes of Mt Pirongia (962 metres). Most tracks head for the moutain's top. Central hut is a good place to spend the night for a two-day tramp into the park.

Raukumara

Located east of the Bay of Plenty, the park is a rugged forested area with limited facilities for the tramper. The most popular route is the east-west traverse — part of this has been cut and three NZFS huts have been built on it.

STATE FOREST PARKS: SOUTH ISLAND

Mt Richmond

With 177,000 hectares, Mt Richmond is the second largest state forest park and a place where experienced trampers can undertake many long-term treks, many in untracked valleys. The park is located between Nelson and Blenheim and contains 34 NZFS huts. The best access is from the southwest by way of Wairau Valley.

Craigieburn

This state forest park includes most of the Craigieburn Range where you can find tussock tops at an altitude of 2000 metres. Longer journeys in Harper and Avoca valleys are possible.

APPENDIX C: ADDRESSES

The following list of addresses may be useful for trampers. Note, however, that these can change from time to time, especially telephone numbers.

NATIONAL PARKS
Chief Rangers

Urewera
  The Chief Ranger
  Waikaremoana
  Private Bag
  Wairoa
  Tel Tuai 803

Tongariro
  The Chief Ranger
  Park Headquarters
  Mount Ruapehu
  Tel 814

Egmont
  The Chief Ranger
  PO Box 43
  New Plymouth
  Tel 80829

Abel Tasman
  The Chief Ranger
  183 Commercial St
  Takaka
  Tel 58026

Nelson Lakes
  The Chief Ranger
  c/o Post Office, St Arnaud
  Tel St Arnaud 816

Arthur's Pass
  The Chief Ranger
  Arthur's Pass National Park
  Arthur's Pass
  Tel 500

Westland
The Chief Ranger
PO Box 14
Franz Josef
Tel 827

Mt Cook
The Chief Ranger
PO Box 5
Mt Cook
Tel 819

Mt Aspiring
The Chief Ranger
PO Box 93
Wanaka
Tel 7660

Fiordland
The Chief Ranger
PO Box 29
Te Anau
Tel 7521

Other field offices
Urewera
Park Ranger Station
Morrison St
Taneatua
Tel 250

Park Ranger Station
Main Rd
Murupara
Tel 641

Tongariro
Park Ranger Station
Ohakune Mountain Rd

Ohakune
Tel 578

Park Ranger Station
Turangi
Tel 8548

Egmont
Park Ranger
Display Centre
Dawson Falls
(Telephone: ask for
Dawson Falls Toll
Exchange)

Abel Tasman
Park Ranger Station
Marahau
RD 2, Motueka
Tel 730 W

Nelson Lakes
Lake Rotoroa Ranger
Station
c/o Owen River Post
Office
Nelson
Tel Murchinson 167 W

Westland
Senior Ranger
PO Box 9
Fox Glacier
Tel 807

Mt Aspiring
Ranger in Charge
National Park Ranger
Station
Glenorchy
Tel 9

Fiordland
Ranger In Charge
National Park Ranger
Station
Clifden
Tel TTE 84 K

**DEPARTMENT OF
LANDS AND SURVEY**
The following district
offices for Lands and
Survey have information
on crown lands and maps
of tracks and parks.

Auckland
PO Box 5249
Auckland 1
Tel 771 899

South Auckland
PO Box 460
Hamilton
Tel 82 489

Taranaki
PO Box 43
New Plymouth
Tel 80 829

Gisborne
PO Box 1149
Gisborne

Wellington
PO Box 5014
Wellington
Tel 725 808

Hawke's Bay
PO Box 148
Napier

Marlborough
PO Box 97
Blenheim
Tel 6079

Nelson
PO Box 443
Nelson
Tel 81 579

Westland
PO Box 123
Hokitika
Tel 585

Invercargill
    PO Box 826
    Invercargill
    Tel 87 334

Canterbury
    Private Bag
    Christchurch
    Tel 799 760

Otago
    PO Box 896
    Dunedin
    Tel 70 650

NEW ZEALAND FOREST SERVICE

The NZFS conservancy or regional offices are good sources of information and handouts for the state forest parks in their area.

Auckland
    Conservancy Office
    PO Box 39
    Auckland 1
    Tel 33 269

Rotorua
    Conservancy Office
    PO Box 1340
    Rotorua
    Tel 80089

Wellington
    Conservancy Office
    Private Bag
    Wellington
    Tel 721 569

Palmerston North
    Conservancy Office
    PO Box 647
    Palmerston North
    Tel 89 109

Nelson
    Conservancy Office
    PO Box 140
    Nelson
    Tel 81175

Westland
    Conservancy Office
    PO Box 138
    Hokitika
    Tel 1225 or 1226

Canterbury
    Conservancy Office
    PO Box 25-022
    Christchurch
    Tel 791 040

Southland
    Conservancy Office
    Private Bag
    Invercargill
    Tel 88 074

The following addresses are for the NZFS district offices that can assist with trip planning in state forest parks.

NORTH ISLAND
Tararua
    District Office
    RD 31
    Manakau
    Tel 572

    District Office
    PO Box 40-440
    Upper Hutt
    Tel 283 922

Pureora
    Park Headquarters
    Pureora
    Tel 870

District Office
PO Box 38
Te Kuiti
Tel 144

Pirongia
    District Office
    PO Pirongia
    Pirongia
    Tel 646

Kaimai-Mamaku
    District Office
    PO Box 12
    Mamaku
    Tel 701

    District Office
    PO Box 1026
    Tauranga
    Tel 87 677

Kaweka
    Ranger in Charge
    Kaweka Headquarters
    Otamauri
    Tel 882

Whakarewarewa
    Park Headquarters
    PO Box 1340
    Rotorua
    Tel 81 165

Haurangi
    Forest Ranger
    Te Kopi
    Cape Palliser Rd, Pirinoa
    Tel 893

Kaimanawa
    District Office
    Private Bag
    Turangi
    Tel 7723

Ruahine
  District Office
  Private Bag
  Woodville
  Tel 7344

Park Ranger
Pohangina Base
RD Ashhurst
Tel Apiti 732

Coromandel
  District Office
  701 Pollen St
  Thames
  Tel 86 772

  Park Headquarters
  Kauaeranga Valley
  RD 2 Thames
  Tel 269 W

Rimutaka
  District Office
  PO Box 191
  Masterton
  Tel 80 060

Raukumara
  District Office
  PO Box 348
  Napier
  Tel 53 129

SOUTH ISLAND
Lake Sumner and Hanmer
  District Office
  Private Bag
  Christchurch
  Tel Culverden 226

  District Office
  PO Box 214
  Hanmer Springs
  Tel 7218

Mt Richmond
  District Office
  PO Box 228
  Blenheim
  Tel 88 099

  District Office
  PO Box 12
  Rai Valley
  Tel 21 D

Craigieburn
  Forest Ranger
  Private Bag
  Darfield
  Tel Springfield 790

Catlins
  District Office
  Wyndham
  Tel 242

North-West Nelson
  District Office
  PO Box 96
  Takaka

  District Office
  PO Box 45
  Westport

The following NZFS
offices can assist trampers
with trips in state forests,
wildlife and scenic reserves
or coastal parks.

South-west Otago Scenic
Reserve
  ·Secretary
  PO Box 896
  Dunedin
  Tel 770 650

  Reserve Ranger
  PO Box 53
  Owaka
  Tel 237

Stewart Island
  Chief Ranger
  PO Box 3
  Halfmoon Bay
  Tel 30

Okarito
  NZFS Office
  PO Box 9
  Harihari
  Tel 435

Waiotapu Forest
  Chief Ranger
  Waiotapu Forest
  Private Bag
  Rotorua
  Tel Rerewhakaaitu 848

Kaingaroa
  NZFS Office
  Murupara
  Tel 714

Waitakere Ranges
  Information Centre
  Scenic Drive
  Arataki
  Auckland
  Tel 817 7134

Herbert Forest
  NZFS Office
  No 9 ORD
  Oamaru
  Tel Herbert 365

Otago Coast Forest
  NZFS Office
  RD 1
  Brighton
  Tel Taieri Mouth 558

Longwood Forest
  NZFS Office
  PO Box 47
  Otautau
  Tel 8423

Red Rocks Coastal Park
    Parks Department
    Wellington City Corpor-
    ation
    Wellington
    Tel 724 599

Great Barrier Is State Forest
    NZFS Office
    Private Bag
    Port Fitzroy
    Great Barrier Island
    Tel 4 K

Tairua Forest
    Chief Ranger
    Private Bag
    Waihi

USEFUL ADDRESSES
The following are other
addresses that trampers
might find handy in plan-
ning their expeditions.

Federated Mountain Clubs
    of New Zealand
PO Box 1604
Wellington

New Zealand Mountain
    Safety Council
c/o Department of Internal
    Affairs
Private Bag
Wellington

National Parks Authority
c/o Department of Lands
    and Survey
Private Bag
Wellington

New Zealand Alpine Club
PO Box 41-038 Eastbourne
Wellington

New Zealand Mountain
    Guides Assoc
PO Box 5132
Wellington

Canterbury Mountain
    Radio Service Inc
PO Box 22-342
Christchurch

Southland Field Radio
PO Box 6054
Invercargill

Wellington Mountain
    Radio Service
PO Box 3468
Wellington

Bibliography

The author is indebted to the following books, pamphlets and guides that aided him constantly during his research of New Zealand tramping.

Abel Tasman National Park, edited by Gordon Cole, Abel Tasman National Park Board, Nelson.

Arthur's Pass National Park, edited by C J Burrows, Arthur's Pass National Park, Christchurch.

Bushcraft, edited by R W Burrell, National Mountain Safety Council of New Zealand, Wellington.

Coromandel: The Holiday Peninsula, by Ian Whalley, Endeavour Publishing.

Egmont National Park, edited by J H Fullarton, Egmont National Park Board, New Plymouth.

Fiordland National Park, edited by Gerald Hall-Jones, Fiordland National Park Board, Invercargill.

Guide to Coromandel State Forest Park, published by the New Zealand Forest Service, Wellington.

Guide to the Great Outdoors, by Roger D Foley, Southern Press Ltd.

Kaimanawa Forest Park Hunting and Recreation Guide, New Zealand Forest Service, Wellington.

Mobil's Guide to North Island, by Diana and Jeremy Poe, AH & AW Reed, Wellington.

Moir's Guidebooks, updated by the New Zealand Alpine Club, Wellington.

Mount Aspiring National Park, edited by W S Gilkison, Mount Aspiring National Park Board, Dunedin.

Mount Cook National Park, edited by H E Connor, Mt Cook National Park Board, Christchurch.

National Parks Accommodation Guide, published for the National Parks Authority by the Department of Lands and Survey, Wellington.

Nelson Lakes National Park, edited by Emily Host, Nelson Lakes National Park Board, Nelson.

New Zealand — a travel survival kit, by Tony Wheeler, Lonely Planet Publications, South Yarra, Australia.

Stewart Island, Department of Lands and Survey, Wellington.

Stewart Island Track and Hut Information, New Zealand Forest Service, Wellington.

Tararua State Forest Park Hunting and Recreation Guide, New Zealand Forest Service, Wellington.

Tararua State Forest Park Route Guide, New Zealand Forest Service, Wellington.

The New Zealand Tramper's Handbook, by Grant Hunter, AH & AW Reed Ltd, Wellington.

This Land is Your Land, Department of Lands and Survey, Wellington.

Tongariro National Park, edited by A E Esler, Tongariro National Park Board, Wellington.

Urewera National Park, Urewera National Park Board, Auckland.

Waikare River Track Guide, Urewera National Park Board, Auckland.

Ways to the Wilderness, by Philip Temple, Whitcoulls Ltd, Christchurch.

Whakatane River Walk Track Guide, Urewera National Park, Auckland.

Africa on the Cheap
Australia — a travel survival kit
Burma — a travel survival kit
Bushwalking in Papua New Guinea
Canada — a travel survival kit
Hong Kong, Macau & Canton
India — a travel survival kit
Kashmir, Ladakh & Zanskar
Kathmandu & the Kingdom of Nepal
Korea & Taiwan — a travel survival kit
Malaysia, Singapore & Brunei — a travel
  survival kit
North-East Asia on a Shoestring
Pakistan — a travel survival kit
Papua New Guinea — a travel survival kit
The Philippines — a travel survival kit
South America on a Shoestring
South-East Asia on a Shoestring
Sri Lanka — a travel survival kit
Tramping in New Zealand
Trekking in the Himalayas
Thailand — a travel survival kit
USA West
West Asia on a Shoestring (formerly Across Asia on the Cheap)

Lonely Planet travel guides are available around the world. If you can't find them, ask
your bookshop to order them from one of the distributors listed below. For countries
not listed or if you would like a free copy of our latest booklist write to Lonely Planet
in Australia.

Australia Lonely Planet Publications, PO Box 88, South Yarra, Victoria, 3141.
Canada Milestone Publications, Box 2248, Sidney, British Columbia, V8L 3S8.
Denmark Scanvik Books, Sankt Annae Plads 30, 1250 Kobenhavn K.
Hong Kong The Book Society, GPO Box 7804, Hong Kong.
India UBS Distributors, 5 Ansari Rd, New Delhi.
Japan Intercontinental Marketing Corp, IPO Box 5056, Tokyo 100-31.
Malaysia MPH Distributors, 13, Jalan 13/6, Petaling Jaya, Selangor.
Nepal see India
Netherlands Nilsson & Lamm bv, Postbus 195, Pampuslaan 212, 1380 AD Weesp.
New Zealand Roulston Greene Publishing Associates Ltd, PO Box 33850, Takapuna,
  Auckland 9.
Papua New Guinea Gordon & Gotch (PNG), PO Box 3395, Port Moresby.
Singapore MPH Distributors, 116-D JTC Factory Building, Lorong 3, Geylang Square,
  Singapore 1438.
Sweden Esselte Kartcentrum AB, Vasagatan 16, S-111 20 Stockholm.
Thailand Chalermnit, 1-2 Erawan Arcade, Bangkok.
UK Roger Lascelles, 16 Holland Park Gardens, London W14 8DY.
USA (West) Bookpeople, 2940 Seventh St, Berkeley, CA 94710.
USA (East) Hippocrene Books, 171 Madison Ave, New York, NY 10016.
West Germany Buchvertrieb Gerda Schettler, Postfach 64, D3415 Hattorf a H.